Life's a Dream

Life's a Dream

Pedro Calderón de la Barca

A PROSE TRANSLATION

AND CRITICAL INTRODUCTION BY

MICHAEL KIDD

University Press of Colorado

Published by the University Press of Colorado
5589 Arapahoe Avenue, Suite 206C
Boulder, Colorado 80303

 The University Press of Colorado is a proud member of
the Association of American University Presses.

The University Press of Colorado is a cooperative publishing enterprise supported, in part,
by Adams State College, Colorado State University, Fort Lewis College, Mesa State College, Metropolitan
State College of Denver, University of Colorado, University of Northern Colorado, and Western State College
of Colorado.

The paper used in this publication meets the minimum requirements of the American National Standard for
Information Sciences—Permanence of Paper for Printed Library Materials.
ANSI Z39.48-1992

Library of Congress Cataloging-in-Publication Data

Calderón de la Barca, Pedro, 1600–1681.
[Vida es sueño. English]
Life's a dream / Pedro Calderón de la Barca ; a prose translation and critical introduction by Michael Kidd.
p. cm.
Includes bibliographical references.
ISBN 0-87081-776-0 (hardcover : alk. paper) — ISBN 0-87081-777-9 (pbk. : alk. paper)
1. Calderón de la Barca, Pedro, 1600–1681. Vida es sueño. I. Kidd, Michael, 1968– II. Title.
PQ6292.V5K5313 2004
862'.3—dc22
2004010260

13 12 11 10 09 08 07 06 05 04   10 9 8 7 6 5 4 3 2 1

 Co-winner of the 2004 Colorado Endowment for the Humanities Publication Prize
The CEH Publication Prize annually supports publication of outstanding nonfiction works
that have strong humanities content and that make an area of humanities research more
available to the Colorado public. The CEH Publication Prize funds are shared by the
University Press of Colorado and the authors of the works being recognized.
The Colorado Endowment for the Humanities is a statewide, nonprofit organization dedicated
to improving the quality of humanities education for all Coloradans.

Para Nicolás—
corónente tus hazañas

If the cave dweller were suddenly to leave the sunlight and go back down
to his old seat in the cave, would his eyes not fill with gloom?
PLATO, *The Republic*

He said, "My Lord knows what is spoken in the heaven and the earth,
and He is the Hearing, the Knowing." "Nay!" say they, "medleys of dreams!
Nay! he has forged it. Nay! he is a poet."
THE KORAN

To be not a man but the figment of another man's dream—
what extraordinary indignity, what bewilderment!
JORGE LUIS BORGES, "The Circular Ruins"

Contents

◈◈◈

Contents

☙❧

Preface

❧

THIS PROSE TRANSLATION of Pedro Calderón de la Barca's *La vida es sueño* is envisioned as both a classroom text and a script for performance, and the accompanying materials reflect that dual function. The Introduction and Glossary are written especially with American high school and university students in mind, whereas the Suggestions for Directors are intended primarily for those interested in taking the play to the stage. The Translator's Notes will appeal to specialists, translators, and others with an interest in Spanish language and poetry or in the details of textual criticism. The Bibliography provides a starting point for anyone who wishes to pursue in greater depth the issues raised in the introductory materials.

The Spanish text used as the basis of the translation is that of J. M. Ruano de la Haza (Castalia, 2nd ed., 2000); all significant divergences from Ruano's text are explained in section 7 of the Translator's Notes. To permit an unencumbered encounter with the play, no footnotes have been used in the body of the translation; all issues of interpretation and necessary clarifications are dealt with in the supplementary materials (see especially Introduction, section 4; Translator's Notes, sections 5–7; and the Glossary). Unless otherwise indicated, all translations of secondary sources are mine.

In preparing this project, I have benefited tremendously from the suggestions and moral support of friends and colleagues, many of whom read some or all of the manuscript. I am particularly grateful to Max Adrien, Jorge Brioso, Anthony Cárdenas, Scott Carpenter, Frederick De Armas, David Eddington,

John Estill, Timothy Face, Jaime Gelabert, Alyosha Goldstein, Pam Hammons, José Ignacio Hualde, Humberto Huergo, John Lipski, Michael McGaha, Rogelio Miñana, Éva Pósfay, Dale Pratt, J. M. Ruano de la Haza, and Cathy Yandell. A special thanks to my wife, Adriana Estill, for her attentive ear and discerning eye. Finally, I am exceptionally indebted to Alfred Rodríguez, my former colleague and mentor at the University of New Mexico, who scrupulously reviewed two completed versions of the manuscript. His expertise, generosity, and spirited engagement will not be forgotten.

—M.K.
Northfield, Minnesota
April 2004

Life's a Dream

Introduction

❧❧

1. SPAIN AT THE TURN OF THE CENTURY (1600)

When Calderón was born in 1600, Spain was the most powerful country in the world, but the seeds had already been planted of a decline that would take it, by the time of his death in 1681, to the humiliating status of a second-tier power. The story of Spain's rise and fall is the sobering tale of a country that collapsed under the burden of its own achievements. Rather than chronicle that process in detail, which would occupy much more space than this Introduction allows, I will begin with three salient general features of early modern Spanish society: religious intensity, inequality before the law, and a deep sense of national pride that suffered serious blows throughout the seventeenth century. These three characteristics are important because they forcefully underpin the ideology of Calderonian Spain and, more broadly, of what is known as the Old Regime, that is, the set of social and political norms that held sway across Europe prior to the French Revolution in 1789. Thus, although none of the characteristics is unique to Spain, they all imply assumptions about the world strikingly different from those that inform modern liberal democracies (including present-day Spain), and their examination will provide an essential preface to the survey of Spanish literature and culture with which I end this section of the Introduction.

❧

CALDERÓN WAS BORN IN AN AGE of deep religious conviction. It may be difficult for westerners of the early twenty-first century, anesthetized by the

1

freedom of worship that all liberal democracies guarantee, to grasp the significance of this fact. Especially in Spain, whose Middle Ages were defined by a long struggle to reunite the peninsula under Christian rule, religious belief was not a matter of choice, and Catholicism permeated all aspects of life and determined the course of history. Even language reflects the omnipresence of religion: to speak Spanish became (and remains) synonymous with speaking "Christian," and official correspondence of the period referred to "both Majesties" in deference to God as well as the king. Early modern Spanish identity, to the extent that one can generalize about it, was forged in a crucible of religiosity that never wavered.

Many of the major events and institutions associated with this period came about as a result of that religiosity. The Spanish Inquisition was founded in 1478 with the purpose of rooting out heresy, especially among Jewish (and later Muslim) converts to Christianity. Unlike the Papal Inquisition, which had been in place in other parts of Europe since 1233, the Spanish Inquisition was placed under almost exclusive control of the Spanish kings; the pope's power was limited to naming the Inquisitor General. Because its jurisdiction was limited to baptized Christians, its power was considerably increased when all unbaptized Jews were forced either to convert or to leave the peninsula in 1492.[1] Also in 1492, the pope honored King Ferdinand and Queen Isabella with the title *Catholic Monarchs* upon their reconquest of Granada, the last independent Muslim kingdom on the peninsula; in 1609 the Moriscos (Moorish converts to Christianity) suffered the same fate the Jews had in 1492. In 1540 Ignatius of Loyola founded the Jesuit Order, dedicated to an active (rather than a speculative) pursuit of faith. The Jesuits provided great impetus to the Counter Reformation, which had come into full swing as Spain united with Rome to stay the rising tide of Protestantism. Costly religious wars between Catholics and Protestants ensued across Europe, exhausting the Spanish treasury in its struggle against countries like England (which it tried to invade) and the Low Countries (part of its Hapsburg patrimony, which it was able to hold only by force) in addition to its traditional Mediterranean rival, France. Finally, a great cost in manpower and wealth was imposed by the evangelization of the indigenous peoples of the Americas.

∾

As MODERN READERS, we also take for granted the legal sanctity of individual equality and political representation, a product of Enlightenment thought that has become the cornerstone of liberal democracy. But in early modern Europe, no such principles existed in practice. A few examples from Calderón's Spain must suffice.

First, the distribution of power was not equitable. At the top, of course, reigned the king and his court. The powerful nobility, concentrated in the countryside, had its own estate in Parliament, as did the clergy, which, along with the military orders (religious in character), wielded considerable influence. A third parliamentary estate was occupied by the major municipalities, which were considerably diverse in structure and tended to represent a democratizing force. Above the municipal level, however, citizens had no political representation; nor was there trial by a jury of peers, for the king was the ultimate arbiter in cases of injustice. Private property was held primarily by the crown and the first two parliamentary estates, whereas the municipalities were allowed to lease land from the crown for public use. Taxation was regressive, with the poor shouldering the burden of contributions to the state treasury. The inferiority of women, peasants, slaves, Indians, and the unbaptized was routinely (although not universally) asserted, and discrimination against such groups not only prevailed but was also legally sanctioned. For example, in the wake of the expulsion of the Jews, as those who chose to convert rather than leave the country began to occupy civil and clerical positions of authority, promulgation began of the famous "pure-blood" statutes—analogous to the English anti-Catholic laws—which excluded anyone of non-Christian lineage from occupying positions of power. The anguish subsequently felt by the many writers and intellectuals of the period who were of Jewish descent became, according to the twentieth-century Spanish historian Américo Castro, a defining feature of early modern Spanish literature.[2]

Despite all these factors, the term *absolute monarchy* gives an incorrect impression of sixteenth- and seventeenth-century Spain, which was actually "one of the freest nations in Europe, with active political institutions at all levels. Remarkably free discussion of political affairs was tolerated, and public controversy occurred on a scale paralleled in few other countries."[3] The fact that the system was inequitable does not mean its inequities were not perceived, and the literature of the period amply documents many diverse perspectives regarding justice and equality. As far back as the thirteenth century, St. Thomas Aquinas (c. 1225–1274) had argued for the radical equality of all human souls, and his principles were now invoked in Spain to defend the rights of Indians and women. Typically, however, such arguments were directed against individuals who abused the system or against particular manifestations of the system rather than against the system itself. This is an important distinction. Men like Bartolomé de las Casas (1474–1566) and Francisco de Vitoria (1492–1546) argued for humane treatment of the Indians, but they firmly supported the effort to convert them to the Catholic faith. Hence the New Laws of 1542—promulgated largely in response to Las Casas's unpublished manuscript, *A Brief Account of the Destruction of the Indies* (*Brevísima relación de la destrucción de las Indias*)—abolished the *encomienda* (the land-tenure system that required the natives to pay rent or to work in exchange for the right to continue living on their ancestral territories), the abuse of which had turned the Indians into de facto slaves.[4]

Teresa of Ávila ("Saint Teresa," 1515–1582), for her part, notes in the first chapter of her autobiography that her father's caring nature led him to pity the plight of slaves (ownership of which was legal throughout sixteenth- and seventeenth-century Europe); yet rather than question the system that permitted slavery to exist, he simply refused to own them himself and treated those owned by others with kindness. Similarly, the lesson that María de Zayas apparently intends to teach her female readers through the harrowing tales of her *Eye-Opening Love Stories* (*Desengaños amorosos,* 1647) is not to rebel against male authority but simply to dissociate themselves from men altogether, as does the character Lisis upon entering the convent at the end of the last story. Finally, regarding the inherent inequality believed to exist between lords and vassals, it is telling that when the peasants of Lope de Vega's *Sheep's Fount* (*Fuente Ovejuna,* 1619) rise up to overthrow and murder their tyrannical master, literally tearing him to pieces, they do so with shouts of "Long live King Ferdinand! Death to evil Christians and traitors!"

Lest there be any doubt, however, the occasional *real* threat to the values of the Old Regime was met with a severity that tended to discourage future attempts: the Comuneros revolt of 1520, the Morisco uprising of 1568, the Catalonian insurrection of the 1640s (in which Calderón himself fought on the side of the king), the Pueblo rebellion of 1680, and so on.

❧

IN MOST PEOPLE'S MINDS, the year 1492 is associated with Columbus's maiden voyage to the Indies, an event that richly deserves all the importance attached to it. Although Columbus (1451–1506)—who was financed by the Spanish crown and wrote his diary in Spanish but was not Spanish by birth (he was born in Genoa and later moved to Portugal)—died insisting he had reached India, it soon became apparent that he had come upon two great continents previously unknown to Europeans. Spain's primary claim to those continents and to whatever riches and natural resources they contained catapulted it almost immediately from its traditional, Mediterranean sphere of influence onto the center stage of European politics, forever changing the course of its history. Eventually, Spain's pretensions in the New World would put it at odds not only with its traditional Mediterranean rival, France, but also with two rising Atlantic powers, Holland and England, toward whom its animosity only grew with the success of the Protestant Reformation.

Columbus's voyage, together with the other momentous events of 1492 and several that soon followed,[5] cemented in Spaniards' identity a proud nationalism bound to a profound sense of manifest destiny. By the seventeenth century, however, national pride was coming under increasing strain. An ominous portent was the catastrophic defeat of the Invincible Armada by the English Navy in 1588. More important, the shiploads of gold and silver that flooded into the country from the New World, much to the envy of Spain's European enemies (and subject to relentless pirate attacks by those enemies), were not nearly enough to finance the staggering military expenditures of the Spanish crown against those same European enemies on the continent; and the treasury was forced to declare bankruptcy at least eight times between 1557 and 1680. At the same time, the influx of American bullion into the peninsula came about without a corresponding rise in productivity, thus creating a galloping inflation that necessitated a seemingly endless series of currency devaluations throughout the seventeenth century, popularly known as the "currency dance" (*baile del vellón*). Intelligent observers interpreted these factors as dire warning of the country's political decline, confirmed in 1648 when the Peace of Westphalia (which ended the Thirty Years' War) formalized Spain's surrender of European hegemony to France. By the time of Calderón's death in 1681, Spaniards could look back to the time of the Catholic Monarchs only with nostalgia, as a golden age of their country's history from which they had been forever expelled.

&

SPAIN'S LITERARY GOLDEN AGE also took root in the time of Ferdinand and Isabella, although it did not reach fruition until much later. In this sense, the year 1492 is yet another milestone. Antonio de Nebrija (1444–1522), a renowned humanist and professor at the University of Salamanca, published in that year his *Grammar of the Castilian Language* (*Gramática de la lengua castellana*), the first grammar of a modern vernacular language, which prophetically argued for the use of Spanish as an instrument of empire. In December of the same year, Juan del Encina (1468–1529), a student of Nebrija's, composed and performed several short nativity sketches, which he called eclogues, in the palace of the Duke and Duchess of Alba outside Salamanca. In the history of Spanish drama, which had no significant medieval tradition upon which to build, these unrefined plays are tremendously important and can be seen as the starting point of an unbroken dramatic tradition that eventually culminates in Calderón and *Life's a Dream*. (More detail on the evolution of Spanish theater is offered in the next section of the Introduction.)

Spanish poetry and prose also flourished during this period. In 1496 Encina published his eclogues together with a treatise titled *Art of Spanish Poetry* (*Arte de poesía castellana*), the first manual of poetry written in Spanish, in which he argues for the beauty and poetic potential of the Spanish language. He was proven right only a few decades later: through incorporation of traditional Italian Renaissance meters, Garcilaso de la Vega (1501–1536) conferred on Spanish poetry a previously unknown prestige. A hundred years later Luis de Góngora (1561–1627), although much maligned during his time, gave seventeenth-century poetry its most unique voice with his sixty-three-stanza *Myth of Polyphemous and Galatea* (*Fábula de Polifemo y Galatea*, 1613). In narrative, landmarks included the anonymous picaresque novel *Lazarillo de Tormes* (1558), a devastating critique of laxity and corruption at all levels of society, as well as the two volumes of Cervantes's masterpiece *Don Quixote* (1605, 1615). Straddling both poetry and prose are the sublime writings of three of sixteenth-century Spain's most intensely spiritual authors: Saint Teresa of Ávila (1515–1582), Fray Luis de León (1527–1591), and Saint John of the Cross (1542–1591)—all of them, significantly, from families of Jewish origin (as were Nebrija, Encina, Góngora, and possibly Cervantes). Of great importance for historiography, finally, is the first generation of New World chroniclers to follow in Columbus's footsteps: Las Casas (1474–1566), Fernández de Oviedo (1478–1557), Cortés (1485–1547), Cabeza de Vaca (c. 1490–c. 1557), and Díaz del Castillo (c. 1495–1584).

By Calderón's time, Spanish literature had assumed a set of characteristics that later critics, borrowing from art history, termed *Baroque.* Formally speaking, the Spanish Baroque in all literary genres employed elaborate or highly stylized syntax, frequent use of Latin- and Italian-based neologisms, and a heavy dependence on greatly exaggerated metaphors and wordplay. The first two of these characteristics are usually associated with the term *culteranismo* and the latter with *conceptismo.* Rather than opposed, as many critics tend to view them, the two phenomena are intricately connected and represent two sides of the coin that is Baroque language, of which the poetry of Góngora is perhaps the prime example. Thematically, Baroque writers came to terms with their disappointment over Spain's political decline by emphasizing the deception and uncertainty of earthly existence, harking back to the biblical view of life as a walk through "the valley of the shadow of death" (Psalms 23 4); such a life was a mere illusion that could be shattered only through the liberating embrace of death. To emphasize the illusory nature of this existence, the Spanish Baroque relied on three central metaphors: life as art, life as theater, and, most important for Calderón, life as a dream.

Apart from literature, Spain's contribution to written culture (I leave aside painting and music) in this period can be grouped into three main areas: theology, philosophy, and science. To begin with, it is instructive to point out that this distinction would not likely have been made in Calderón's time, which considered philosophy and science as two branches (one theoretical, the other practical) of the same tree of knowledge. Theology, furthermore, given its perceived relationship to truth, had been thought of in the Middle Ages as the "Queen of the Sciences" and was still referred to that way in Cervantes's *Don Quixote,* although its popularity as a course of study notably declined in the Renaissance.[6]

In Spain, as in the rest of Europe prior to the Protestant Reformation, theology owes its existence to scholasticism, the peculiarly medieval attempt to imbue faith with rational content. Scholasticism was perfected in the thirteenth century by Thomas Aquinas through a harmonization of Christian dogma with the philosophical principles of Aristotle, whose entire corpus, thanks largely to scholars working in Spain, had just been translated into Latin from Arabic. (Previously, only the early works of Aristotle had been available in Latin.) In Spain, the scholastic method continued to be the basis of important writings in theology throughout the Renaissance, and the universities in Salamanca and Alcalá de Henares were major centers of scholastic thought. The rational subtleties and nuanced details characteristic of Calderonian drama, in fact, owe much to scholasticism's influence.

Scholastic-based theology was given new impetus in Spain by the Council of Trent (1545–1563), which convened to deal with Protestantism at a theological level and was dominated by Spaniards in its closing years. The council's pronouncements, reached through classic scholastic debate, neatly summarize the essence of Catholic theology and elucidate its major points of conflict with Protestantism. Of particular importance for the interpretation of *Life's a Dream,* the council reaffirmed the traditional view of *justificatio* (transformation of the sinner from a state of unrighteousness to one of holiness) through the exercise of individual free will; this view contrasted sharply with Protestantism's (especially Calvinism's) emphasis on salvation by predestination. Predictably, the council also upheld the authority of popes and councils in the determination of doctrine, whereas Protestantism gave sole authority to the Bible. The council reaffirmed the number of sacraments at seven, which Protestants had reduced to two; and it reiterated that the sacrament of communion implies the transubstantiation of the body of Christ in the communal bread and wine. The council also upheld belief in purgatory, the use of indulgences (although it called for an end to obvious abuses), the worship of saints, and the veneration of relics and icons.[7] All these dogmatic points surface in Calderonian drama.

Because scholasticism always subjects reason to faith, it is not philosophy in the sense that we know it today. For many years, however, the conclusions of philosophy and theology were considered complementary and compatible, one focused on the natural order and the other on the supernatural order. Yet by the Renaissance, a new metaphysics permitted a break between theology and philosophy. A major result of this break was political philosophy, best exemplified by Machiavelli's *The Prince* (1513). In its exclusive concern with the history and government of human affairs, Machiavelli's treatise represented a radical departure from the theocentrism of medieval thought.

In Spain, where Machiavelli never took deep root (despite the fact that *The Prince* based its model of the ideal ruler on the shrewd policies of King Ferdinand), an interesting blend of traditional scholasticism and the daring new political philosophy is found in the writings of Francisco Suárez (1548–1617). Considered the last of the great scholastic thinkers, Suárez was also at the forefront of political thought in his defense of the concept of national sovereignty. In his Latin treatise *On the Defense of Faith* (*De defensio fidei*, 1613), he rejected the divine right of kings and insisted that political power resided in the people. Even more radical is the position of Juan Mariana (1536–1624), whose book *On Kings and Kingship* (*De rege et regis institutione*, 1599) defended the right of the people to murder despotic kings. The response to both Suárez's and Mariana's works, especially abroad, was dramatic. *On the Defense of Faith* was burned in London; *On Kings and Kingship* suffered the same fate in Paris. Neither book was banned in Spain, however; the crown tolerated such writings presumably because it assumed they were directed toward the Protestant monarchies of northern Europe, which it had an interest in undermining. In any case, because the authors of both treatises were Jesuits, it is almost certain that Calderón was familiar with their ideas and, moreover, that he addressed those ideas in *Life's a Dream*.

Another branch of thought that had a profound impact on early modern society, if not on philosophy itself, was Humanism, the educational program initiated by Petrarch and based on the rigorous study of ancient Greek and Latin texts. Because Humanist approaches to ancient texts required a thorough knowledge of Greek and Latin, it was only a matter of time before they were applied to the New Testament—originally written in Greek but transmitted throughout the Middle Ages in Latin—as well as to theology and canon law, written exclusively in Latin. In his momentous *Treatise Against the Donation of Constantine* (*Declamazione contro la Donazione di Constantino*, 1440), for instance, the Italian scholar Lorenzo Valla—relying on a knowledge of Latin that Humanism had taught him—demonstrated that the document known as the Donation of Constantine, on which the church based its rich patrimony and territorial claims to Italy, was a forgery. Valla was only the first of many Humanists who would inevitably bring to the surface the many errors and contradictions buried in Christianity's long stewardship of textual transmission. As the

Spanish Humanist Hernán Núñez so aptly explained over a century later (1566), "[W]hen a humanist corrects an error in Cicero, for example, the same error has to be corrected in Scripture."[8]

Such methods obviously represented a serious threat to the church's authority, and thus the tools of Humanism—in a way many Humanists would never have wished—precipitated and bolstered the claims of the Protestant Reformation. Nowhere is this contradiction more evident than in the remarkable life and work of Thomas More (1478–1535). More's early association with prominent Humanist and reform-minded circles in England earned him a recognition that would ultimately gain him entry into the inner circle of King Henry VIII. But More, always a faithful Catholic, refused to support Henry's divorce from Catherine of Aragon and the resulting break with Rome; and the king had him beheaded for his opposition.

In Spain, Humanism flowered in the late fifteenth and early sixteenth centuries in figures like Antonio de Nebrija and Juan del Encina (see above, p. 6). Before the Protestant Reformation, the church supported the goals of Humanism and even sponsored the University of Alcalá's publication of the Polyglot Bible (1514–1517), which contained the first New Testament printed in Greek. After the Reformation, however, as Spanish authorities watched the rapid advance of Protestantism across Europe, Humanism came to be identified with the Reformation, and the position of Humanists became untenable. This was especially the case with the brand of Humanism associated with the great Dutch scholar Erasmus (c. 1466–1536), who had made a particularly profound impact in Spain. In 1530 an outstanding Spanish Humanist, Juan de Valdés (c. 1510–1542), fled the country for Italy to avoid arrest related to his *Dialogue of Christian Doctrine* (*Diálogo de doctrina christiana,* 1529), which smacked of Erasmian influence. Three years later, in a chilling letter written to Juan Luis Vives[9] from Paris, Rodrigo Manrique, son of the Inquisitor General, commented on the state of the country from which both now lived in exile:

> You are right. Our country is a land of pride and envy; you may add, of barbarism. For now it is clear that down there one cannot possess any culture without being suspected of heresy, error and Judaism. Thus silence has been imposed on the learned. As for those who have resorted to erudition, they have been filled, as you say, with great terror. . . . At Alcalá they are trying to uproot the study of Greek completely.[10]

Manrique's letter is uncannily prophetic. The Council of Trent, among its other rulings, soon reaffirmed the sole authority of the Vulgate (the Latin Bible) in an attempt to insulate it against the tools of classical philology that Humanism espoused; it also rejected Humanist education for priests even though clerical education was widely acknowledged to be in desperate need of reform. From this point on, to be a Humanist in Spain almost certainly meant rousing the ire of the Holy Office. This was the case of Fray Luis de León, who, besides authoring some of the sixteenth century's most beautiful poetry (see above, p. 6), was also an excellent scholar of Hebrew at the University of Salamanca. Ignoring the council's wishes regarding the Vulgate, he insisted in his classes on the authority of the Hebrew Bible, for which he was ultimately denounced and imprisoned. By the time Calderón wrote *Life's a Dream*, Humanism had been virtually extinguished—although not forgotten—in Spain, eclipsed by its ideological opposite, neostoicism. Best represented in the brilliantly sardonic writings of Francisco de Quevedo (1580–1645) and in striking contrast to Humanism's optimism and engagement, neostoicism counseled detachment and resignation as remedy to the disillusioned reality of seventeenth-century Spain.

Regarding the early modern scientific tradition in Spain or the lack thereof—Spain produced no equivalent to Copernicus (1473–1543), Galileo (1564–1642), Kepler (1571–1630), or Newton (1642–1727)—one must bear in mind two important points. First, Spanish science was dominated early on by Jews and Jewish converts to Christianity; their persecution, consequently, was one of the factors that negatively impacted the scientific tradition in Spain.[11] Second, a series of restrictive measures taken in 1558–1559 as part of the Counter Reformation, although not intended to impede scientific development, could not but negatively impact it. The measures included a formalization of censorship procedures, leading to the publication of the first Index of Prohibited Books; a ban on the importation of foreign books; and a prohibition against teaching or studying at foreign universities.[12] The last measure was particularly harmful, considering that 25 percent of the 228 scientific authors who flourished in Spain at the beginning of the sixteenth century (prior to the ban) had studied abroad.[13] With these facts in mind, we can now turn to the individual disciplines.

Spain was never at the vanguard of original work in theoretical mathematics. Its most important sixteenth-century contribution, Juan Pérez de Moya's

Practical and Speculative Arithmetic (*Aritmética práctica y especulativa,* 1562), is entirely derivative. The situation did not change in the seventeenth century, even though in the rest of Europe this was the age of coordinate geometry (Descartes), differential calculus (Newton), and integral calculus (Leibniz). Whether the poverty of the Spanish mathematical tradition was a consequence of the association that, as Américo Castro has suggested, early modern Spaniards made between the exercise of the intellect and the impurity of blood (i.e., intellectuals were identified with Jews) matters little.[14] Whatever the cause, the result was far-reaching: "[W]ithout a basis in mathematics there can be no astronomy or physics with a scientific grounding, and thus the physics that was taught in [Spanish] universities continued to be Aristotelian, a mass of philosophical abstractions not only without relationship to reality but also, in many occasions, closed to reality and experimentation."[15]

These attitudes explain why the works of key figures such as Copernicus, Galileo, Kepler, and Newton were not widely understood in Spain even though they were available. Copernicus, in fact, was on the reading list at the University of Salamanca when Calderón studied there in the early seventeenth century. And yet the Spanish view of the universe, which forms the basis for Vasily's astrological predictions in *Life's a Dream,* continued to follow that outlined by Ptolemy in the second century A.D. At its center lay the earth: fixed, immobile, and immediately surrounded by the other three primal elements (water, air, and fire). At a greater distance, eight concentric spheres hung in suspension. The first seven spheres contained, respectively (in order of proximity to the earth), the moon, Mercury, Venus, the sun, Mars, Jupiter, and Saturn. The eighth sphere, called the firmament, contained the fixed stars and constellations. Beyond it, an unseen "prime mover" (*primum mobile*), to which all the spheres were tethered, revolved around the earth once every twenty-four hours, dragging everything along with it.

In addition to the stagnating effect it produced on astronomy, the lacuna in theoretical mathematics helps explain why modern philosophy, so dependent on theoretical mathematics (Descartes's work in geometry, for example, was crucial to his philosophical principles), never flowered in Spain. In contrast, Spaniards were at the forefront of applied math and science. Driven by the imperative to explore and conquer the New World, cartography achieved great distinction in Spain, and Pedro de Medina's *Art of Navigation* (*Arte de navegar,*

1545) is a key text in which the Atlantic Ocean assumes an outline very close to reality. Cartography was complemented by work in natural history, that is, the cataloging of the flora and fauna of the Americas, as evidenced in early chroniclers such as Fernández de Oviedo (see above, p. 7) and in later ones such as Francisco Hernández, a physician appointed by Philip II in 1570 to lead the first modern scientific expedition to the New World. Spain also led the way in reforming the old Julian calendar. A Spaniard, Pedro Chacón, was among the three authors of the final document that Pope Gregory XIII approved in 1582— the import of which, judging by the jokes made in *Life's a Dream,* was still remembered in Calderón's time. When Philip II founded, during the second half of his reign (1556–1598), Madrid's Academy of Mathematics—whose mission was entirely practical in nature—he confirmed the Spanish preference for the applied sciences.

An important fruit of this preference was medicine, which flourished in the first half of the sixteenth century in figures such as Pedro Jimeno, who in 1549 published his discovery of the third bone of the inner ear. The enigmatic figure of Miguel Serveto (a.k.a. Michael Servetus, 1511–1553) also deserves mention in this context. Born in Navarre, Serveto seems to have fled Spain some time after the publication of a heretical theological treatise, *On the Errors of the Trinity* (*De Trinitatis erroribus,* 1531), which disputed the nature of the Trinity. He resettled in France, studying medicine in Paris and Montpellier, and became quite distinguished in anatomy. Convinced that the soul resided in blood, he was the first to discover the principles of pulmonary circulation. Serveto's theological views, despised by Catholics and Protestants alike, eventually caught up with him, and he was arrested in Geneva and burned at the stake by order of Calvin.

Even with the restrictive measures of 1558–1559, the end of the century still produced several Spanish figures worthy of note, such as the surgeon Francisco Díaz, whose treatise on kidney disease in 1588 is considered a foundation of modern urology. And in 1575, Juan Huarte de San Juan published his monumental *Assessment of Intellectual Endowments* (*Examen de ingenios para las ciencias*). An intriguing, multifaceted treatise that confirms the pre-Enlightenment permeability of the disciplinary boundaries now imposed between medicine, philosophy, and political science, Huarte's work was based on the idea that the faculties of the soul as well as one's professional inclinations are influenced by the four bodily humors. It had an enormous impact on the development of psychological profiling of literary characters in the following century, and Calderón was almost certainly familiar with it.

The theory of the four humors on which Huarte's treatise is based provides an excellent opportunity to examine the state of scientific knowledge and the modes of rational thought current in the seventeenth century. Like the Ptolemaic view of the universe, the theory of the bodily humors dates back to the ancient world, specifically to the Greek physician Galen (second century A.D.). It posits a body composed of four basic humors, each associated with a certain temperament. In the healthy individual blood predominates, but a disproportionate rise in one of the other humors brings about an ailment related to the characteristics associated with that humor. By the Renaissance, each humor had become linked through analogy to a series of other paradigms such as the four elements of which all matter was believed to be composed, as shown in Figure I.1.[16]

FIG. I.1 RENAISSANCE VIEW OF THE COSMOS

Humor	*Temperament*	*Primary Qualities*	*Element*	*Age*	*Season*	*Planet*
blood	sanguine	hot, moist	air	childhood	spring	Jupiter
phlegm	phlegmatic	cold, moist	water	middle age	autumn	moon
choler*	choleric	hot, dry	fire	youth	summer	Mars
melancholy†	melancholic	cold, dry	earth	old age	winter	Saturn

* yellow bile; † black bile

The connections between the different parts of this elaborate system served as a guide to interpreting man's relation to the cosmos, which was viewed as an organic, meaningful whole: hence Sigismund's reference to man as "a world unto himself" in act 2 of *Life's a Dream* (p. 119). The theory is thus important not only because of its prevalence but also because it demonstrates the great gap between a rational process predisposed to draw connections based on analogies and surface similarities and that of the modern scientific method, which seeks to break down and classify on the basis of natural physical laws and inherent characteristics.

The intellectual background of Calderón's play is living testament to the period in which these two fundamentally opposed scientific approaches were engaged in an active contest for legitimacy. Indeed, the play's reliance on the Ptolemaic universe and the theory of the four humors shows that although certain intellectual fields undoubtedly suffered in Spain as a result of the Counter Reformation, what we now call the pseudosciences—alchemy, astrology, chronology, the study of emblems—all flourished. It is almost as if, along with literature—which reached its maximum brilliance *after* the restrictive measures of 1558–1559—the pseudosciences became the prime expression of the creative energies that no longer found an outlet in philosophy, the natural sciences, or even theology (after the Council of Trent's pronouncements, which it took to be definitive, the church preferred to consider closed any discussions regarding dogma). The only thing left to do with received knowledge was to popularize it, and this was the role now assumed by the public theater, whose greatest representatives—Lope de Vega, Tirso de Molina, and Calderón—were all men of the cloth. We can now consider their dramatic formula in some detail.

2. THE SPANISH COMEDIA

Comedia is a generic term used to refer to Spanish secular drama—whether tragic or comic—in the sixteenth and seventeenth centuries: the most prolific national theater in the history of world literature. Its history dates back to Juan del Encina, who, as noted earlier (p. 6), performed his first eclogues in the palace of the Duke of Alba in December 1492. Encina's early eclogues were nativity pieces, but the evolution of his theater coincided with extensive visits to Italy, inviting a gradual secularization that culminated in a veritable glorification of classical mythology in the *Eclogue of Plácida and Vitoriano* (*Égloga de Plácida y Vitoriano,* 1513; banned by the Index of Prohibited Books in 1558). Encina's contemporaries—Bartolomé de Torres Naharro, who spent a significant amount of time in Italy as well, and Gil Vicente, a Portuguese national who often wrote in Spanish—also contributed to the secularization of the theater.

Encina's generation of playwrights is characterized by the courtly venues of its performances and the noble standing of its spectators. By the mid-sixteenth century, following successful tours of several Italian theater companies through the peninsula, a more middle-class theater audience began to develop. A key figure during this period was Lope de Rueda (d. 1565/1566), whose success as an actor and owner of a theater company led him to write his own plays as well. In the 1570s, immediately prior to the success of Lope de Vega's new dramatic formula, a brief experimentation with tragedy (especially Senecan tragedy) appeared in figures such as Juan de la Cueva and Cristóbal de Virués. By this point, however, popular tastes had invaded the early aristocratic framework of Spanish theater, and the narrow precepts of classical tragedy found less fertile soil in Spain than they had in Italy and France.

At this point Calderón's immediate predecessor, Lope de Vega (1562–1635, often referred to simply as "Lope"), entered the scene and consolidated the tradition into a fixed formula that, insofar as the public theater is concerned, forever vindicated popular over aristocratic sentiment. In his *New Art of Writing Plays in This Age* (*Arte nuevo de escribir comedias en este tiempo*, 1609), presumably written as a defense against those who would attack his populism, de Vega outlines the general formula of his dramaturgy, by now assiduously followed throughout Spain: plays are divided into three acts and written exclusively in verse; they assign primacy to plot, which is to be dizzying in detail; they freely mix serious and comic elements; they disregard what were known as the classical unities[17] and frequently employ subplots; and they tend to eschew tragic denouements in favor of happy and often moralizing endings. Thematically, de Vega's formula draws from history and legend, Italian drama and novellas, classical mythology, the Bible, and the lives of saints; and the subject matter is generally presented as realistically as the highly condensed plots will allow. The themes of love and honor are particularly privileged, and tension between the two often gives rise to the plays' basic conflicts. Honor in particular seems to have had something of a cathartic effect on audiences, as de Vega's own words in *New Art* attest: "Issues of honor work best because they move everyone deeply."[18]

By the time Calderón began writing plays, the immense success of de Vega's formula had assured its hegemony—although it can be argued that Calderón perfected the formula by introducing more economical plots, greater subtlety of thought, and, in some cases, deeper character development. As is the case with *Life's a Dream,* moreover, his plays often include an important allegorical or preternatural dimension designed to test moral and philosophical premises, and thus they are not always best served by rigorously realistic or literal interpretations.

The ideology of the Comedia tends to be conservative by contemporary standards, as it naturally reflects the values of the Old Regime outlined in the previous section. However, I believe it is a mistake to go as far as those who, like José Antonio Maravall, wish to see it merely as a tool used by the state to solidify its own interests.[19] Such views ignore the fundamental power of the artist to resist authority. In Counter-Reformation Spain, of course, few writers would have risked open critique of royal power, although such a stance was tolerated, as we have seen, in the Jesuit writings of Suárez and Mariana (see above, p. 9). Calderón had to be particularly careful because his livelihood was intimately connected to and dependent on the court of Philip IV. But the best writers of any period state their case subtly rather than overtly, and I firmly believe that *Life's a Dream,* on one level at least, represents a subtle critique of certain practices of the Hapsburg monarchy (see below, pp. 30–32, for more detail).

The language of the Comedia is a product of the exclusive verse format in which it is written. Tellingly, playwrights of Calderón's period were known as poets rather than dramatists; consequently, all poetic figures, including many of the excesses of Baroque poetry, were incorporated into drama. Metaphor in particular was stretched to the limit through the use of *conceptismo* (see above, p. 7). Many verse forms were cultivated, but the conventional eight-syllable verse in assonant rhyme, a favorite of the traditional ballad, predominated. When read aloud, this form does not stray far from the rhythms of prose and was easily understandable in the oral context of performance. Furthermore, audiences were accomplished listeners and spoke of going to "hear a play" rather than to see it, demonstrating the great gulf that separates them from present-day patrons of theater (not to mention those of film).

In fact, in the primary importance it assigned to plot and to the spectator's ability to listen, classical Spanish drama was closer to the principles of Aristotelian theory than the lack of tragic elements would first lead one to believe. Aristotle noted that plots "ought to be so constructed that, *even without the aid of the eye,* he who hears the tale told will thrill with horror and melt to pity at what takes place."[20] Whereas Lope de Vega and Calderón were less concerned with provoking horror and pity in the spectator—although it is significant that Rossaura mentions precisely these two elements after overhearing Sigismund's first monologue (see p. 94)—it is clear that for them, as for Aristotle, elements such as costume, scenery, and special effects (what Aristotle called "spectacle") were secondary. As a consequence, staging techniques were, as in Shakespeare's

England, extraordinarily simple. By the 1560s—the period associated with Lope de Rueda and the beginnings of a middle-class dramatic ethos—public plays were being performed in the courtyards (*corrales*) of hospitals run by charitable institutions (*cofradías*), where space and mobility were limited. The first permanent public theaters arose around 1580, just as Lope de Vega's formula was taking hold.[21] Similar in blueprint to the hospital courtyards, the permanent theaters were built in the inner patios of preexisting buildings; hence they continued to be known as *corrales*. They attracted rowdy, heterogeneous audiences that were segregated by class and sex. (Actresses, by contrast, were from the beginning allowed onstage alongside actors.) Although more advanced than the hospital courtyards, they still did not favor elaborate staging techniques; and, being open air like the courtyards, they were at the mercy of the elements.

Beginning in the early 1980s, the outstanding work of three theater historians in particular—J. E. Varey, J. M. Ruano de la Haza, and John J. Allen—has considerably advanced our understanding of the seventeenth-century Spanish stage and allowed us to reconstruct its details. A platform stage, about six feet high and roughly twice as long as it was deep (a common ratio was 12' by 24'), projected into the audience. On the two ends were lateral platforms that could be used for seating in more conventional productions or as an additional staging area if required. Across the back of the central stage, and perhaps extending along the lateral platforms, ran a permanent five-story structure commonly referred to as the *vestuario* (dressing room) because the basement level, hidden from the audience's view, served as the men's dressing area (as well as a space for managing special effects) whereas the stage level provided access to the women's dressing room. Balconies with detachable railings projected from the second and third levels and were supported by two sets of columns that rose from the stage. The top level, hidden in an attic area, housed stage machinery.

Each of the *vestuario*'s three exposed tiers, which measured about eight feet tall and several feet deep, was curtained off and divided horizontally (superficially by the columns and internally by thin partitions) into three separate sections. This arrangement created a total of nine independent, recessed cells that could be used for a variety of scenic effects. The left and right curtains of the bottom tier generally served as the main entrances and exits, whereas the middle curtain (but sometimes the left or right one) could be drawn back to reveal a "discovery space" such as an allegorical setting, a cave, or a prison. The second tier of the *vestuario* could be used to play balcony or window scenes; the third tier might represent additional windows, the top of a castle wall, or a mountain peak. Mountains could be simulated, with varying degrees of realism, by a ramp leading from one of the balconies onto the lateral platforms or, alternatively, onto the center stage providing it did not block access to the lower-tier entrance and exit curtains. In principle, any of the nine niches could be used as a discovery space or "inner stage," creating a dynamic, multidimensional flexibility that often led to an inversion of natural spatial relationships.

Because the plays were performed in broad daylight (local statutes prohibited night shows), the recessed niches of the *vestuario* would have provided a distinct lighting contrast to the brighter surroundings of the main stage. Costumes, gestures, and textual cues were used to compensate for the general lack of scenery, requiring a strong suspension of disbelief on the part of the audience to complete the theatrical illusion. Although Italian innovations in set design had made possible more elaborate staging techniques by the time Calderón wrote *Life's a Dream,* the limited stage directions of the text appear to call for little beyond the description just offered. As Ruano de la Haza concludes in his excellent reconstruction, "[W]ith the help of the curtains, a simple background décor and one spatial inversion, *La vida es sueño* was probably staged . . . simply, efficiently, with a minimum of disruption and without unduly straining either the imagination or the credulity of the audience."[22] (More ideas regarding the staging of *Life's a Dream* are offered in the Suggestions for Directors.)

In conclusion, it is worth noting that the formulaic structure of the Comedia favored prodigious output. De Vega's biographer, Juan Pérez de Montalbán, claims he wrote an astonishing 2,000 plays, of which "only" around 500 have survived (in contrast to the 38 we possess of Shakespeare). Tirso de Molina (1583–1648), author of the original Don Juan play, claimed over 400 dramatic works, of which about 80 are known today. The balance of Calderón's literary production includes 108 full-length secular plays, 73 short allegorical plays, and a few isolated poems and interludes. Although the formulaic structure of the genre led to a number of ill-conceived plots and some tenuously developed characters, many of the plays are still worthy of study; and the best of them rank with the best of Shakespeare. Among the latter, Calderón's *Life's a Dream* is the undisputed gem.

3. CALDERÓN THE MAN: A BRIEF CHRONOLOGY

1598—The Spanish throne passes from Philip II to Philip III, the first of the Hapsburg kings to actively patronize the theater. The golden age of Spain's dramatic tradition, under the leadership of Lope de Vega, is in full swing.

1600–1606—Calderón is born on January 17, 1600, to noble parents in Madrid, the third child of six. In 1601 his family moves to Valladolid, where the Spanish court has briefly relocated. By 1606 both he and the court are back in Madrid to stay.

1608–1613—Following his father's wishes that he become a priest, Calderón receives an excellent Jesuit education at the Colegio Imperial of Madrid, where he masters Latin and learns the rudiments of New Testament Greek.

1610—Calderón's mother dies giving birth to her last child (which also dies). The event may be behind the horrific description of Sigismund's birth in *Life's a Dream* (pp. 102–103).

1611—Francisco, an illegitimate son of Calderón's father, who has lived with the family with only the father aware of the blood relationship, is banished from the household and disinherited; at the same time, Calderón's sister Dorotea (age thirteen) is sent to a convent in Toledo, and his brother Diego (sixteen) is entrusted to the care of a relative in Mexico. When the father dies four years later, Francisco's biological relationship to the family is revealed, and his banishment is explained as punishment for an act of violence. One critic has seen in these events an attempted rape of Dorotea by Francisco with the possible collusion of Diego, instilling in Pedro a horror of incest that haunts several of his works including *Life's a Dream*.[23]

1614—Calderón enrolls in the University of Alcalá. His father remarries.

1615–1620—Calderón's father dies in 1615; his will reveals an authoritarian character that may have informed the troubled relationship between Vasily and Sigismund in *Life's a Dream*. His father's death prompts Pedro to interrupt his studies at Alcalá because of a fight with his stepmother over the inheritance, which is finally settled in 1618. Calderón abandons his plans of becoming a priest and continues his education at the University of Salamanca, where he studies law, history, theology, and philosophy, receiving his degree in canon law. In 1620 he composes a sonnet for a literary contest and is mentioned favorably by Lope de Vega.

1621—In the spring, Philip IV ascends to the throne, initiating a lavish patronage of the theater that will ultimately shower Calderón with attention. In the summer, Calderón and his brothers are accused of murdering a servant of the high constable of Castile; seeking refuge in the house of the German ambassador, they are eventually convicted and forced to pay a crippling fine to the victim's father.

1622—Calderón again composes poems for various literary contests.

1623—Calderón writes his first play, *Love, Honor, and Power* (*Amor, honor y poder*). Some biographers suggest he may have spent several years around this time in the service of the king in Milan and Flanders, but it has proved impossible to document such assertions.

1629—An enraged Calderón pursues the assailant of one of his brothers (it is not known which) into the Convent of the Trinitarians in Madrid, where he joins several ministers of justice in irreverently stripping the nuns of their veils and searching their cells in a futile hunt for the aggressor. Lope de Vega, whose daughter Marcela is a member of the convent, complains of the incident in a letter to the Duke of Sessa. The famous court chaplain, Father Hortensio Félix Paravicino de Arteaga, delivers a sermon in which he uses the incident as a pretext to attack playwrights. Calderón is later placed under brief house arrest for poking fun at Paravicino in a passage from his play *The Steadfast Prince* (*El príncipe constante*). According to Ruano de la Haza, an early version of *Life's a Dream* was fully under way by this point.

1633—Calderón writes *Devotion to the Cross* (*La devoción de la Cruz*), an unsettling and highly influential play that centers on the incestuous desire of a brother and sister who are unaware of their relationship, recalling the events of 1611.

1635—On St. John's Eve (June 23), Calderón stages an elaborate production of *Love, the Greatest Enchantment* (*El mayor encanto, amor*). The play is performed before the king on a floating stage, designed by the Florentine engineer Cosme Lotti, in the pond of the Retiro Park in Madrid. Calderón also writes *Secret Affront, Secret Vengeance* (*A secreto agravio, secreta venganza*) and *The Doctor of Honor* (*El médico de su honra*), two deeply disturbing works about jealous, honor-driven husbands who murder their wives on the basis of suspicion and innuendo, recalling Shakespeare's *Othello*.

Lope de Vega's death in August confirms Calderón's supremacy in the theater.

1636—Calderón publishes, with significant personal involvement, many of his most important works in *Comedies, Part One* (*Primera parte de comedias*), in which *Life's a Dream* is assigned first place in the order of plays. He is named Knight of the Order of Santiago by Philip IV. Documentation suggests that an allegorical version of *Life's a Dream* was performed in the village of Fuente el Saz for the Feast of Corpus Christi.[24]

1637—Calderón writes *The Wonder-Working Magician* (*El mágico prodigioso*), the chilling tale of a student of metaphysics who sells his soul to the devil to win the woman he desires.

1640s—A difficult period for the playwright on all levels, this decade is marked politically by the uprising in Catalonia, in which Calderón participates (on the side of the king) in 1641–1642. As the revolt continues unabated, a somber mood takes hold in Madrid. The moralists, long enemies of the theater, succeed in severely restricting performances. The queen's death in October 1644 furthers their cause, and public theaters are closed (as was customary) in an act of mourning. The prince's death almost exactly two years later (October 1646) extends the closure until the king remarries in 1649; theaters are then reopened but never recover the spirit of the 1620s and 1630s. In stark contrast to the more than forty plays he penned during the previous ten years, Calderón's literary production throughout the 1640s amounts to fewer than ten works. One of his most important, however, is probably from this period: *The Mayor of Zalamea* (*El alcalde de Zalamea*), a searing indictment of abuse of power and the resulting erosion of boundaries between public and private life. Also during this period, Calderón fathers an illegitimate child, Pedro José (the mother's identity remains unknown), who dies by age ten. Calderón initially calls the boy his nephew but confesses the real relationship when he is ordained; he makes almost no reference to the child in his writings.

1651—This year marks a turning point in Calderón's life: he suffers a serious illness, witnesses the death of both his brothers as well as his mistress, and decides to be ordained a priest, belatedly fulfilling his father's wishes. From this point until his death on May 25, 1681, Calderón devotes all his energies to composing short allegorical plays based on Catholic theology (*autos sacramentales*) and extravagant mythological pieces for the court. In 1673, eight years before his death, he writes an allegorical version of *Life's a Dream* (perhaps a revision of the one performed in 1636).

4. *LIFE'S A DREAM*: ANALYSIS AND INTERPRETATION

(Those not already familiar with *Life's a Dream* are encouraged to postpone reading this section until finishing the play itself.)

Love, dishonor, vengeance. Kingship, loyalty, rebellion. Knowledge, control, choice. Dreams, illusion, reality. These are the themes that haunt *Life's a Dream* and make it the peer of such plays as *Oedipus* and *Hamlet.* That Calderón's play belongs with Sophocles's and Shakespeare's atop the dramatic canon is also reflected in the sheer volume and diversity of the critical response it has inspired, as documented by Jesús A. Ara Sánchez's superb annotated bibliography (see Bibliography, section 5), to which I am heavily indebted in the preparation of these pages. The immensity of this secondary literature and its heterogeneous, often conflicting content prevent any exhaustive treatment in this Introduction. Instead, I have limited myself to a brief survey of three levels of analysis that I consider crucial to the play's interpretation—the human, the political, and the philosophical—along with a sampling of the bibliography most relevant to each area (regardless of whether the references cited corroborate my own readings).

ॐ

THE HUMAN LEVEL OF *LIFE'S A DREAM* informs the play's basic dramatic structure through an intense interrogation of the boundaries of traditional social and familial roles, giving pride of place to the themes of love, honor, and vengeance that so thrilled audiences of the Comedia. As king, Vasily has sought to rob Sigismund of his birthright to the throne; as father, he has acted toward him in a way that "denied me my humanity," as the prince furiously exclaims in act 2 (p. 118). The first action is unlawful, for kings have a duty to educate princes in a manner that prepares them for governing. The second act is immoral, for Christians have a duty to raise their children with compassion and understanding. Sigismund is consequently consumed with rage and a desire for revenge, expressed in a remarkable passage in which he dreams out loud that "Clothold shall die by my hands! My father shall kiss my feet!" (p. 130).

The prince's dream emphasizes the archetypal similarities between the story of Sigismund and the myth of Oedipus, popularized in antiquity by the Greek playwright Sophocles and the Roman dramatist Seneca (the latter, a favorite of Calderón, is mentioned by Vasily at the end of his long speech at court in act 1 [p. 104]). In both stories a father, in attempting to avoid fulfillment of a prophecy that predicts his overthrow by his own son, ends up precipitating the events he wishes to avoid. In the Greco-Roman plays, Oedipus unknowingly kills his father and, again unknowingly, marries his mother. In *Life's a Dream,* Sigismund symbolically kills his mother when she dies giving birth to him, and, as the passage quoted in the previous paragraph demonstrates, he desires to humiliate his father.[25] A disastrous outcome is averted only when the king, recognizing his error, decides to confront his fate rather than run from it. This act enables— without requiring—Sigismund's conversion and points the play toward a happy end.

Like Sigismund, Rossaura has never known her father, Clothold, who abandoned her mother, Viola, and violated his secret marriage vow to her. Rossaura now faces an eerily similar situation as she finds herself abandoned by her lover, Aistulf, Duke of Muscovy, who has left her to claim the Polish throne. Unlike Sigismund, Rossaura is hindered by her sex. With no known male guardian to avenge her dishonor, she must disguise herself as a man and seek justice on her own. Her arrival in Poland brings her into contact with the prince, who is spellbound by her beauty even as she is dressed as a man.

Rossaura also meets Clothold, and, probably suspecting he is her father, speaks a series of double entendres that, as Ruano de la Haza suggests in the Introduction to his edition of the play,[26] are aimed at forcing a confession from him: "You have given me, sire, my life," she tells him after he frees her and Bugle at the end of act 1 (p. 105). When this approach fails, she reveals her gender to him in a further appeal for his help; especially if she suspects he is her father, this move would have struck her as a particularly effective way to gain his support, for her sex places a special obligation on her father as her only male relative. Indeed, Clothold recognizes his debt to Rossaura in an aside but refuses to admit it to her directly. Furthermore, he is unwilling to act publicly on her behalf because the Spanish honor code dictated that the dishonor of an unmarried daughter also disgraced her closest male guardian. He is further handicapped when he becomes indebted to the duke for saving him from the wrathful Sigismund, and, ultimately, all he can offer Rossaura is life in a convent. She rejects his offer and pleads to the prince. At this point the two threads of the plot are united as the symbolically orphaned protagonists come together in their struggle for justice, both fighting against their fathers in the chaos that envelops the country in act 3.

It is surprising that Rossaura, as one of the play's more complex characters, has not generated more critical interest.[27] Her male disguise in act 1 and her strong will and independent streak throughout the play recall several of Shakespeare's most famous comic heroines. Like Viola in *Twelfth Night* and Rosalind in *As You Like It*, Rossaura proves attractive to the opposite sex even while dressed as one of them; like them and like Portia in *Merchant of Venice* (another cross-dresser), she also displays great ingenuity and wit as she maneuvers through a male-dominated world, particularly in her bold confrontations with Clothold and Aistulf. Such actions make for highly captivating drama and might even be taken as a sign that Calderón believed in some degree of equivalency between the sexes; but any such interpretation must be balanced by several important facts.

First, Rossaura leaves Poland to search for Aistulf only at the suggestion of her mother, Viola, who gives her Clothold's sword—a symbol of male authority—knowing that he, as Rossaura's closest male guardian, is the only one who can legitimately restore her honor; the masculine disguise is simply a means of ensuring safe passage to Poland so the plan can be put in motion. Second, when Clothold proves unable to assist Rossaura in the way she desires (by killing the duke), she recognizes that her plan to take matters into her own hands is "madness" and "self-destruction" (pp. 141–142). Third, what ultimately convinces Aistulf to marry Rossaura is not the latter's feminine independence but rather the male authority of Sigismund and Clothold. Finally, Rossaura accepts a solution that reunites her with the very man who abandoned her and whom she, just one scene earlier, had threatened to kill.[28] None of these points, however, detracts from the sympathy and depth of Rossaura's characterization.

Rossaura's sidekick Bugle is a less complex figure, governed by many of the traits commonly associated with servants of the period: self-interest, intolerance for physical hardship, loquaciousness (hence his name), quick wit, and a certain intuition that appears to have allowed him to deduce the real relationship between Rossaura and Clothold, as he suggests in act 3 (p. 148). Although it is unclear precisely when or how he made this connection, he hints at it when, at the beginning of act 2, he blackmails his way into the service of Clothold, who evidently perceives him as enough of a threat to order his imprisonment along with Sigismund at the end of act 2. Officially, Clothold might justify Bugle's incarceration as a reason of state: to prevent him from exposing Aistulf's role in Rossaura's dishonor and thus spoiling the king's plans for the duke. Unofficially, if Clothold suspects that Bugle has inferred his relationship to Rossaura, jailing him also becomes a convenient way to silence him and thus protect Clothold from the dishonor that would stain him as Rossaura's closest male guardian. At any rate, Bugle's syllogistic conclusion that he is being punished for having kept quiet (p. 133)—in contrast, he insists, to the typical servant—rings a bit hollow and perhaps serves to preempt sympathy over his sudden and surprising death two scenes later (servants rarely die in the Comedia). His demise, furthermore, proves useful in confirming the king's recognition that he has caused the current chaos by attempting to avoid it.[29]

The other relationship of note in the play is that of Aistulf and Stella. First cousins who have never met, they harbor competing claims to the Polish throne, and their initial exchange, far from following the protocol of the period, is charged with sly innuendos and double entendres. Aistulf, for example, compares Stella's gaze to a comet that lights the night sky: regal and spectacular but also whimsical and fleeting, not to mention that in antiquity comets were frequently associated with calamity and especially with the fall of kings.[30] They agree to marry as a peaceful solution to their conflicting claims to the throne, revealing the importance of arranged marriage among royal families and also perhaps hinting at the Hapsburg propensity toward intermarriage. The revelation of Sigismund's existence throws the plan into doubt, however, and Rossaura destroys it for good when, employed as Stella's lady-in-waiting, she makes a fool out of Aistulf in front of the princess. The matter is settled only when Sigismund restores Rossaura's honor by forcing Aistulf to marry her. Thus the duke is punished for his arrogance, losing the crown he had so relentlessly pursued. In a final insult, Sigismund offers his own hand in marriage to Stella, whom Aistulf must now watch inherit the throne without him. This act of poetic justice, which ostensibly cements the play's happy end, nevertheless leaves a nagging suspicion regarding a marriage between relatives (Sigismund and Stella). A discussion of the work's political and historical dimensions will clarify this point.

&

ON A POLITICAL LEVEL, *Life's a Dream* demonstrates the vulnerability of the institution of monarchy in the early modern era, especially in transitional periods when there was no clear heir apparent or when, as in the play, there were several competing claims to the throne. By laying bare this Achilles heel of monarchy, Calderón raises important questions about the role of kingship and about the limits of knowledge and power. Aistulf's observation to Stella that Vasily is "more inclined to academic pursuits than to women" (p. 100) is not to be taken lightly. The pursuit of academic questions is fine for academics, but in a king, who should be concentrating on the affairs of state—part of which includes ensuring and properly raising a legitimate heir—it is a serious error. When, moreover, academic pursuit comes to dictate the affairs of state, as when Vasily's astrological predictions determine the prince's barbaric education, the results prove catastrophic.

Vasily is punished for his foolishness with a civil war that divides the country. On one side is the mob that liberates Sigismund from prison, described by the king as "willful and reckless" (p. 138) and by Clothold as "impulsive and blind" (p. 139). Perhaps because of the historical rivalry between Russia and Poland or perhaps because of the common people's traditional role in monarchy—as guarantor of legitimate succession—the mob strongly prefers the natural heir to the throne, the Polish Sigismund (despite his obvious incompetence), to the foreign-born Duke of Muscovy. Against the mob stands the aristocracy, which supports the king's brokered solution. Even though, as noted earlier (p. 9), the Jesuit treatise of Father Mariana authorized popular rebellions against tyrannical kings (or against more benign kings who, like Vasily, made tyrannical decisions), Calderón knew he was dealing with an explosive issue given his close connections to the court of Philip IV. His dilemma was how to use a popular rebellion to punish the king's error without appearing to justify popular rebellion per se.

At the center of the problem is the extent to which monarchy must be absolute. The issue is concisely summarized in Sigismund's exchange at court with Servant 2: "[Sig.] When the law isn't just, the king needn't be obeyed. [Serv. 2] It wasn't for him to decide whether it was just or not" (p. 114); later, in his dream at the end of act 2, Sigismund goes even further in asserting that "[a] proper prince is he who punishes tyrants" (p. 130). The prince's words clearly reflect the treatise of Father Mariana, whereas the servant's imply an unquestioning loyalty that is best embodied in Clothold, who prefers to die rather than betray the crown: "You would wage war against your father, but I cannot counsel you or come to your aid against my king. I am at your mercy; kill me," he tells the prince when the latter is liberated from the tower in act 3 (p. 137). It matters not that Clothold disagrees with the king's tyrannical act; as a vassal he considers himself bound by the laws of fealty and, for the same reason, is prepared in act 1 to kill Rossaura even knowing that she is his offspring.

Clothold's conflict is similar to the one Shakespeare develops between John of Gaunt, Duke of Lancaster, and his son Harry Bolingbroke, Duke of Hereford. Lancaster, even with the knowledge that the king is guilty of murder, refuses to accuse him openly: "God's is the quarrel; for God's substitute, / His deputy anointed in his sight, / Hath caused his death; the which if wrongfully, / Let heaven revenge, for I may never lift / An angry arm against his minister."[31] Harry, by contrast, ends up overthrowing Richard and proclaiming himself Henry IV. That a legitimate monarch should be so boldly overthrown provoked such controversy in Shakespeare's time that the lines in which Richard loses his crown were omitted in all sixteenth-century texts of the play (and perhaps in performance).[32]

Calderón attempts to contain such controversy in several ways. First, the instigators of the rebellion are identified as "outlaws and peasants," as the soldier tells Sigismund at the beginning of act 3 (p. 135). Second, Sigismund asks his father's forgiveness at the end of the play and even offers him his life. Finally, the soldier who led the rebellion and liberated Sigismund from prison is punished with life imprisonment by Sigismund himself. This final act has struck many critics as excessively cruel and ungrateful, but to leave the rebel soldier unpunished or, worse, to reward him for his rebellion (as he requests) would be to strike openly at the very foundation of monarchy: the notion of the king as "God's substitute" and, hence, the idea that his word must never be questioned. Although Calderón may have been critical of royal power, he could not have risked such a brazen affront to royal authority.

Another way Calderón attempts to contain the potential impact of the theme of rebellion is by setting the play in Poland. If the plot could be interpreted—at least in part—as unique to a remote country that lay, in most Spaniards' minds, at the margin of the civilized world, then there was less chance that it would be seen as applicable at home. Although any quasi-exotic setting might seem to satisfy this condition, the choice of Poland in particular is not gratuitous. The fact that there were three Polish kings named Sigismund (see Translator's Notes, pp. 57–59) suggests a closer connection. Sigismund I fought intermittently with Vasily III of Moscow, whereas Sigismund III invaded Russia and held Moscow for two years. These events, although not paralleled explicitly, are echoed in the play in the prince's rivalry with his father Vasily, a common Russian name (Basilio in Spanish), and with the duke, a Muscovite. Furthermore, Poland's reconversion to Catholicism was one of the great successes of the Counter Reformation, thanks in no small part to Sigismund II who, among other measures, introduced the Society of Jesus (the Jesuits) in 1565. What better country in which to set Sigismund's ostensible triumph of free will (Catholicism) over Vasily's foolish belief in predestination (Protestantism)?

From a Catholic perspective, however, the prince's triumph is somewhat vitiated by the fact that the king, whose obsession with "subtle mathematics" (p. 101) is based on the Ptolemaic system, represents the old order of knowledge that the Counter Reformation wished to preserve (or reinstate)—and this in the country that gave birth to Copernicus, no less. In this way the play foregrounds the clash between the two approaches to science outlined earlier (pp. 14–15). Vasily's defeat at the hands of Sigismund, who in some sense represents the new philosophy of Descartes (see below, pp. 33–34), parallels the threat that the Copernican system represented to the old order—a threat made resoundingly clear by the church's public condemnation of Galileo (a follower of Copernicus) in 1633. Calderón's excellent university education almost certainly provided him with enough background to draw these connections, and one critic even suggests that he could have become aware of further historical details through contact with ambassadors at the court of Philip IV.[33] At any rate, his gift for subtlety allows him to emphasize the more evocative contours of history without forcing them toward facile resolution or bogging the play down in detail.

Although Calderón makes few specific references to Poland's geography, at least two critics have identified the mountainous setting of the prince's tower with the hilly, forested terrain around Krakow.[34] One passage that has caused much controversy is the scene in act 2 in which Sigismund throws the servant "from the balcony to the sea below" (p. 117). Some editors, following a footnote in Juan Eugenio Hartzenbusch's Spanish edition of *Life's a Dream*,[35] have asked whether Poland bordered the sea in Calderón's time. In fact, prior to the partitioning of the country at the end of the eighteenth century, Poland had always possessed a port on the Baltic Sea; moreover, during the reign of Sigismund II, Poland formed a commonwealth with Lithuania (1569) that effectively pushed its boundaries to the Black Sea. Hartzenbusch's misunderstanding may stem from that fact that at the time he was writing (1848), Poland was a landlocked country. The real question, however, is how the Polish royal palace, which before 1596 was located in Krakow and afterward in Warsaw (neither a seaport), could have been conceived of as bordering the ocean.

One critic suggests that Calderón's Baroque fondness for exaggeration led him to magnify the River Vistula into the sea in the same way he turned the hills around Krakow into mountains.[36] Another points out that the reference to the sea would not have struck readers of the period as odd because many of them associated the seventeenth-century Polish state with the naval policies that King Wladislaus IV pursued from 1632 until his death in 1648.[37] Some of the play's Spanish-language editors feel that Calderón should not be held to strict geographical accuracy and that natural features such as the mountains of act 1 and the sea of act 2 are more literary than real.[38] I believe the truth lies at an intersection of all these opinions: Calderón intends the play's geographical references to represent Poland; but, recalling the subtlety with which he employs references to Polish history, he is interested in broad, evocative allusions with some basis in reality rather than in letter-of-the-law accuracy.

In addition to its Polish echoes, *Life's a Dream* may reflect Spain's own past. At the beginning of the reign of Philip II (1556–1598), considerable uncertainty existed regarding the issue of succession. Philip's first wife, the Portuguese Infanta Maria, gave birth to a son, Charles, who early on showed signs of mental instability and had to be excluded from affairs of state or any position of authority. Moreover, the prince "had several violent fits, engineered bizarre plans to escape, and even plotted against his father. Finally in January 1568 Philip ordered him to be arrested and confined; an action taken, as he explained to the pope, 'with sorrow and grief, since he is my only son and first born.' Six months later [Prince Charles] died in confinement."[39] Are we to see in Sigismund a reminder of this sad episode? A limited but significant number of critics has said yes.[40] But would Calderón have been drawn to the event for any reason other than its inherent dramatic appeal?

The question becomes all the more intriguing when one considers that Prince Charles, like many Hapsburg offspring, was the product of poor mixing of the gene pool, for Maria was Philip's first cousin. Although such marriages were not considered incestuous and were actually quite common among all social classes of Calderón's time, they were (and still are) considered by the Catholic Church to be a diriment impediment to marriage as far as the fourth degree of kinship (i.e., first cousins), and special dispensation is required to perform them. Furthermore, astute observers such as Calderón may have intuited what modern genetics has confirmed: that close inbreeding tends to produce offspring who, like Prince Charles, are mentally or physically unfit.[41] For his fourth wife, in fact, Philip II chose his niece, Ana of Austria, twenty-two years younger than he—a union that produced the incompetent Philip III, whose reign coincided with the playwright's youth. As both a faithful Catholic and a court insider with a vested interest in the institution of monarchy, Calderón may have felt strong opposition to such marriages on both religious and political grounds; furthermore, he appears to have had an unusually strong revulsion to incest based on an obscure event from his childhood that has been plausibly reconstructed (see the entry for 1611 in the previous section, p. 20).

In light of such facts, I believe Calderón's peculiar choice of the name Clorilyn for the king's sister (p. 100) and wife (p. 102) is more than an error or oversight, although that is the way many editors and translators have preferred to view it (see Translator's Notes, n. 47). On the contrary, the repetition of the name is significant regardless of whether it is interpreted to mean that Vasily married his actual sister. If he did, then the intertextuality of the story of Oedipus (see above, p. 24) as well as the allusions to the myths of Prometheus and Uranus—all of which involve incest and end in tragedy—could be interpreted as a sinister reflection of the king's own actions and as a warning of the possible consequences.[42] Are these the "details that have no place here" to which Aistulf mysteriously refers in act 1 (p. 100)? If the two Clorilyns are one and the same, furthermore, then Sigismund and Stella—who end up marrying at the end of the play—are half siblings, possibly even full siblings given that we are never told who Stella's father is and must at least entertain the possibility that it is Vasily. Finally, even if the name Clorilyn is understood to refer to two separate women, the uncanny repetition could be taken as an indication that the king, in true Freudian fashion, married someone who *reminded* him of his sister, that is, a substitute. In this case the dark omens that foreshadow the prince's birth and his repeated identification with monstrosity would take on new meaning, as a sign of the king's suppressed incestuous desire.[43]

Interestingly, the Prince Charles legend has inspired a long line of literary works, perhaps the most famous being Friedrich Schiller's *Don Carlos,* in which another pseudoincestuous desire is manifested, in this case between the prince and his stepmother, Elizabeth of Valois. Do such works somehow confirm or build upon Calderón's transformation of the first-cousin kinship between Philip and Maria into the mysterious relation between Vasily and Clorilyn?[44] In any case, the coincidences between Sigismund and Prince Charles—both the products of an incestuous or symbolically incestuous marriage, both judged unfit to govern, both locked away in prison, both conspirators against the king—are too numerous to overlook; and I believe that on one level *Life's a Dream* represents a veiled critique of the deleterious effects of endogamy, which the Hapsburg monarchy (like all European monarchies of the period) routinely practiced.[45] The fact that the "happy ending" of *Life's a Dream* is cemented by a marriage between first cousins (Sigismund and Stella)—perhaps between siblings—comes as final confirmation of this interpretation. Like the traces of Polish history in the play, those that point to Spain's own past deserve more attention than they have received from commentators, who have generally been more interested in the work's philosophical and religious implications.

༄

YET THE FOCUS ON THE INTELLECTUAL CONTENT of *Life's a Dream* is not misplaced, for the play represents the fruit of a mature mind's wrestling with the deep philosophical and religious issues of its time. The play's very title echoes a profoundly unsettling question that has often preoccupied Western philosophy and that even today has no satisfactory answer. As Sigismund asks in act 3, "Are pleasures so akin to dreams that the real ones are taken for lies and the fake ones for authentic? Is there so little difference between the true and the false that it's debatable whether what is seen and enjoyed is real or made up?" (p. 146). Might we be simply the figments of someone else's imagination or the characters of someone else's dreams, as in Jorge Luis Borges's short story "The

Circular Ruins" ("Las ruinas circulares," 1942)? In Calderón's time the question was a favorite among Baroque writers (see above, p. 7), having been foregrounded by the advance of science, the spread of Protestantism, and the rapid decline of Spain's European hegemony—all of which seemed to represent a threat to previously accepted truths. In considering Calderón's response to this question, embodied in *Life's a Dream,* it is instructive to compare it to René Descartes's *Discourse on Method,* published only a year later.

In investigating the nature of reality, Descartes formulates a skeptical approach that begins with the mind as the basis of existence—hence his famous axiom "I think, therefore I am," which goes on to become the cornerstone of modern philosophy. Descartes's approach is revolutionary because, at least in its first step, it rejects everything outside the self, including God. Although Descartes later affirms God's existence through classic scholastic arguments, he does so as a *second step.* This distinction may seem like splitting hairs, but it is crucial to an understanding of the conservative character of Calderón's philosophical approach, which, in *beginning* with a sure knowledge of God's existence and a firm conviction regarding all the doctrinal points of Catholicism, remains essentially medieval and scholastic.

In making this point, however, one must distinguish Calderón's perspective as creator of *Life's a Dream* from that of Sigismund as its main character. The process Sigismund employs to arrive at a knowledge of reality may, in fact, be compared to the Cartesian method precisely because it depends on a radical doubt that deeply marks the prince's character. "What is life? A frenzy. What is life? A vain hope, a shadow, a fiction. The greatest good is fleeting, for all life is a dream and even dreams are but dreams" declares Sigismund in his famous soliloquy at the end of act 2 (p. 132). This Cartesian doubt has interesting parallels in Shakespeare's *Hamlet,* as when the protagonist finds himself paralyzed by deep skepticism regarding the legitimacy of his father's ghost:

> Yet I,
> A dull and muddy-mettled rascal, peak
> Like John-a-dreams, unpregnant of my cause,
> And can say nothing—no, not for a king
> Upon whose property and most dear life
> A damned defeat was made. Am I a coward? . . .

The spirit I have seen
May be the devil, and the devil hath power
T'assume a pleasing shape; yea, and perhaps,
Out of my weakness and my melancholy—
And he is very potent with such spirits—
Abuses me to damn me.[46]

Yet whereas Hamlet ultimately resolves his doubts by staging a play "[w]herein [to] catch the conscience of the King,"[47] even at the very end of *Life's a Dream* Sigismund harbors the sinking feeling that "one day I shall awaken to find myself locked away in my cramped prison" (p. 152).

Such gnawing doubt is inconceivable in the minds of Calderón's spectators because the play's fundamental dramatic irony makes them privy to a perspective that is beyond Sigismund's reach. And although the prince's doubts about reality are almost certainly meant to parallel the audience's own experience in the real world, in the audience's case such doubts are more literary than real, reflecting an old, popular metaphor that becomes central to the Spanish Baroque and that again finds a parallel in Shakespeare: "We are such stuff / As dreams are made on, and our little life / Is rounded with a sleep."[48] Life is a dream, a pitiful imitation of eternity, filled with confusion and despair, from which we must awaken (that is, die) in order to experience things as they really are (i.e., eternity); this is the basic meaning of the contrast between the Spanish terms *engaño* (deception) and *desengaño* (a coming to awareness of that deception) that was so dear to Calderón and his contemporaries. Moreover, because we may awaken at any moment—for death can come when we least expect it—we must always live according to Christian principles and be on guard against temptation lest we risk condemnation.

Before such truths as these, Calderón's play offers no doubt of the Cartesian type for the spectators, who, although they may compare the confusion experienced by the prince to the uncertainty of their world, remain certain of their uncertainty; that is, they remain certain of the essential dividing line between dreams (this life) and reality (the eternal). The protagonist, by contrast, doubting to the very end, remains something of a Cartesian; and this curious tension between the inner and outer perspectives on the action of the play goes unresolved. Thus, whereas Calderón hints at a radical new epistemology confirmed by Descartes the following year, he takes care to do so in a character whose perspective is severely limited. The medieval marriage of philosophy and theology is strained but not broken.

What is the role of the stars in this picture? Far from being an arcane theological matter, the thrust of this question is one that, in slightly different terms, continues to spark fierce debate today and whose definitive answer continues to elude us—at least as of yet. Simply put, the issue is this: to what extent is human choice mediated—by genetics, by environmental factors, or, yes, even by the stars (the widespread existence of astrology columns in the twenty-first century necessitates inclusion of the latter term)? In short, to what extent is *free will* free?

By Calderón's time, the Catholic Church had long recognized that astrology could predict events and measure one's inclinations, and it is noteworthy that all of Vasily's predictions in *Life's a Dream* are ultimately fulfilled. But two crucial points must be added to this observation. First, as in the many misinterpretations of the oracle in Greek tragedy (including the Oedipus plays), Vasily accurately foresaw the outcome or *effect* of events but misinterpreted the *cause* (a scholastic distinction), failing to see that he himself, in the barbaric way he proposed bringing up the prince, was precipitating precisely what he was attempting to avoid. Sigismund points this out in act 3 when he asks: "If anyone were told, 'One day you will be killed by an inhuman beast,' would it be a good solution to wake one up while it was sleeping?" (p. 150). In the second place, the church categorically refuted and prohibited what was called "judiciary" astrology—which counseled remedies that could be taken to avoid the fulfillment of prophecy—because such measures undermined the concept of free will so important to Catholic dogma. This is precisely Vasily's error, which Sigismund again clarifies: "Foreseeing a danger doesn't mean you can protect yourself or guard against it before it occurs; yes, you can always take a few humble measures to protect yourself, but not until the moment is upon you, for there's no way of forestalling its arrival" (p. 151). In short, the stars can influence the future but cannot determine it outright. The point is brought home when Sigismund—contrary to all expectations—apparently repents at the final moment, affirming Catholicism's emphasis on the redemptory power of individual free will.[49]

One may, however, question the sincerity of Sigismund's sudden "conversion," viewing it as the product of a cynical *desengaño* and the culmination of a calculated quest for power in the spirit of Machiavelli's *Prince*. This is the play's last major unresolved question and, together with the related issue of Sigismund's incarceration of the rebel soldier, the one that has most divided critics.[50] On the one hand, a sincere conversion would foreground the legitimacy of Catholic doctrine. On the other, a cynical grab for power, although it would not *negate* the legitimacy of Catholic doctrine, would be more in line with the critique of the Hapsburgs suggested earlier (p. 32). Yet just as in the question of Clorilyn (is she or is she not Vasily's sister?); in that of Vasily's defeat (positive from a Catholic perspective because it refutes judiciary astrology, negative because it marks a threat to the old order); and in that of the difference between dreams and reality (clear to the spectators, hazy to the prince even at the end of the play), Calderón rejects a facile solution to this problem and leaves all doors open. The issue of Sigismund's conversion has no easy answer and, in truth, leaves much to the discretion of the director, for there are no stage directions to indicate the prince's manner or gestures at this crucial moment (see the Suggestions for Directors for ideas on staging this scene). That *Life's a Dream* resists final closure in this way is one mark of its enduring vitality; that it leaves the question in the hands of directors is a sign of its inherent dramatic value; that it does so within the formulaic structure of the Comedia, where happy ends are the norm, is final proof of the subtlety of the author's genius.

෴

ANY INTERPRETATION OF *LIFE'S A DREAM,* however brief, would be incomplete without a reference to the image of the hippogriff, a crucial symbol not only because it is the first word in the Spanish original but also because it unites so many of the play's themes. Rossaura uses the word to allude to the swiftness of the horse that has just thrown her, for the hippogriff is, among other things, a horse with wings. But its symbolism comprises more than just speed. As the unlikely product of a horse (*hippos* in Greek) and a griffin (itself a combination of an eagle and a lion), the hippogriff is "monstrous" in the strict sense of the word: a chaotic union of naturally irreconcilable elements, a blurring of boundaries that many of the play's characters incarnate through an extension of the three basic themes studied earlier. On a personal level, the dishonored Rossaura, forced to take vengeance into her own hands, is half man, half woman, as her disguise in act 1 suggests. Sigismund, because of the savage conditions of his upbringing (and perhaps also because he is the product of incest), is half man, half beast. On a political level, the civil war that engulfs the country stems from the fact that the Vasily is half king, half astrologer whereas Aistulf is half Polish, half Muscovite. Even at the philosophical level, the blurring of boundaries between dreams and reality reaffirms the omnipresent symbolism of the hippogriff. It is altogether fitting, then, that some semblance of order is restored in the last scene of the play only after the king, rejecting Aistulf's advice, refuses to flee upon the "swift miscarriage of the wind" (p. 149) that catapulted Rossaura onto the stage in scene 1.[51]

NOTES

1. One estimate is that 175,000 Jews fled Spain in the spring and summer of 1492 and another 100,000 converted by the August deadline (Gerber 1992, p. 140 [Bibliography, section 7]). The total population of Castile and Aragón at the time was somewhere between 8 and 9 million (O'Callaghan 1975, pp. 604–605 [Bibliography, section 7]).

2. See especially Castro 1954, 1972 (Bibliography, section 7).

3. Kamen 1985, p. 99 (Bibliography, section 7).

4. The lax enforcement of the New Laws, however, led Las Casas to denounce the situation in 1552 by publishing his manuscript, which he dedicated to Prince Philip (soon King Philip II) to assure his awareness of the abuses.

5. For example, Spain's defeat of France and the consequent consolidation of its Italian possessions, confirmed in the Battle of Pavia (1525), and, upon the inheritance of the Spanish throne by Charles of Ghent (Charles I of Spain, Charles V of the Holy Roman Empire) in 1516, the addition of the German lands and the Low Countries to its European possessions.

6. By the seventeenth century, law students outnumbered theologians by over twenty to one in Salamanca and Valladolid (Kamen 1991, p. 154 [Bibliography, section 7]). Hence in the passage from *Don Quixote* alluded to, Don Diego laments the fact that his son, a student at the University of Salamanca, refuses to study theology (part 2, chapter 16).

7. See Ozment 1980, pp. 407–408 (Bibliography, section 7), for more detail.

8. Quoted in Kamen 1991, p. 188 (Bibliography, section 7).

9. Another outstanding Spanish humanist, 1492–1540, friend of Erasmus and tutor to Princess Mary of England, who was forced to flee Spain at age seventeen when the Inquisition burned his parents for being Judaizers (his mother, already dead, was disinterred for the occasion). The entirety of his works was written in exile in England, France, and Flanders.

10. Quoted in Kamen 1991, p. 117 (Bibliography, section 7).

11. López Piñero 1979, p. 77 (Bibliography, section 7).

12. There is some dispute as to the extent of the university ban. One historian notes that exceptions were made for certain colleges in Bologna, Rome, Naples, and Coimbra (Kamen 1985, p. 78 [Bibliography, section 7]). Another asserts that, in the second half of

the sixteenth century, distinguished Spaniards were found in universities throughout Italy, Flanders, and France (Elliott 1963, pp. 223–224 [Bibliography, section 7]).

13. López Piñero 1979, p. 141 (Bibliography, section 7).

14. See especially Castro 1972 (Bibliography, section 7).

15. Domínguez Ortiz 1973, p. 389 (Bibliography, section 7).

16. The diagram is adapted from Murillo 1990, 22 (Bibliography, section 7).

17. Time, place, and action. Thought in the Renaissance to have been mandated in Aristotle's *Poetics* (which mentions time and action but not place), strict observation of the unities is actually a product of postclassical criticism.

18. Vega Carpio 1989, vv. 327–328 (Bibliography, section 3).

19. See Maravall 1990 (Bibliography, section 8).

20. Aristotle 1961, p. 78 (Bibliography, section 3), emphasis added.

21. The first permanent public theater was the Corral de la Cruz, built in Madrid in 1579. The Corral del Príncipe followed in 1582, also in Madrid.

22. Ruano de la Haza 1987, p. 58 (Bibliography, section 8).

23. Parker 1982 (Bibliography, section 8).

24. Pérez Pastor 1905, pp. 98–99 (Bibliography, section 6).

25. On the Oedipal resonances of *Life's a Dream,* see especially Valbuena Prat 1956; Parker 1966; Rozik 1989; Molho 1993, pp. 240–248 (Bibliography, section 8).

26. Ruano de la Haza 2000, pp. 49–57 (Bibliography, section 2).

27. Among the few studies focused on Rossaura, those of Whitby 1960, Lavroff 1976, and Bueno 1999 deserve special mention (Bibliography, section 8).

28. The great gulf that separates Rossaura's attitude from modern feminist sensibilities becomes apparent in Laird Williamson's adaptation of the play (2001 [Bibliography, section 1b]), which rewrites the ending to have Rossaura refuse Aistulf's hand and offer it instead to Sigismund.

29. For more on Clarín, see Bandera 1971 (Bibliography, section 8).

30. Ruano de la Haza 2000, p. 66 (Bibliography, section 2).

31. *Richard II* 1.3.37–41. All Shakespeare references are from the Norton edition (Greenblatt 1997 [Bibliography, section 3]).

32. Greenblatt 1997, pp. 943–944 (Bibliography, section 3).

33. Ginard de la Rosa 1881, pp. 296–297 (Bibliography, section 8).

34. Brody 1969, p. 43; Ziomek 1983, p. 992 (Bibliography, section 8).

35. Hartzenbusch 1918, p. 8n (Bibliography, section 2).

36. Brody 1969, p. 43 (Bibliography, section 8).

37. Strzalko 1959, p. 644 (Bibliography, section 8).

38. Morón Arroyo 2000, p. 137n; Ruano de la Haza 2000, p. 169n (Bibliography, section 2).

39. Kamen 1991, p. 123 (Bibliography, section 7).

40. Schevill 1903; Cotarelo y Mori 1914; Levi 1920; Millé y Giménez 1925; Lieder 1930; Ferdinandy 1961; Alcalá-Zamora 1978 (Bibliography, section 8).

41. That a knowledge of modern genetics (i.e., genetics since the discovery of the structure of DNA in 1953) would not have been necessary for Calderón to intuit the

negative consequences of inbreeding is clear from the following statement, which appears in the article "Consanguinity" published by the *Catholic Encyclopedia* in 1908 (Bibliography, section 5): "Nature itself seemed to abhor the marriage of close kin, since such unions are often childless and their offspring seem subject to grave physical and mental weakness (epilepsy, deaf-muteness, weak eyes, nervous diseases), and incur easily and transmit the defects, physical or moral, of their parents, especially when the interbreeding of blood-relations is repeated" (qtd. from the on-line version). As evidence, the article cites multiple sources including an Encyclical of Pope Gregory XVI from 1836.

42. On the Prometheus myth in *Life's a Dream,* see, for example, Ginard de la Rosa 1881; Morales San Martín 1918; Valbuena Prat 1956; Navarro González 1977 (Bibliography, section 8). On Uranus, see Ruiz Ramón 1990 (Bibliography, section 8).

43. On Clorilyn and the issue of incest, see especially Vida Nájera 1944; Feal and Feal-Deibe 1974; García Barroso 1974; Rodríguez López-Vázquez 1978; De Armas 1986, pp. 111–113; Molho 1993, pp. 240–248; Soufas 1993; Sullivan 1993 (Bibliography, section 8).

44. Rank 1992 (Bibliography, section 8) offers a fascinating study of the incest motif in world literature, including a significant discussion of the Prince Charles theme; see especially pp. 33–50, 99–118.

45. Another interesting parallel occurs in Shakespeare's *Hamlet,* where Claudius, upon murdering his brother the king and inheriting his crown, marries his widow, to whom he refers as "our sometime sister, now our queen" (1.2.8)—meaning, of course, "sister-in-law."

46. *Hamlet* 2.2.5 [3 510, 575 580. On the Cartesian parallels of *Life's a Dream,* see, for example, Ginard de la Rosa 1895, p. 130; Riquer and Valverde 1958, pp. 375–376; García Bacca 1964; Sullivan 1979; Resina 1983; Bradburn-Ruster 1997 (Bibliography, section 8). Comparisons between *Life's a Dream* and *Hamlet* (although not from a Cartesian perspective) are drawn by Blanco Asenjo 1870; Abel 1963; Morón Arroyo 1990 (Bibliography, section 8).

47. *Hamlet* 2.2.582.

48. *The Tempest* 4.1.156–158. See Rupp 1990 and Zaidi 1996 for recent comparisons of *Life's a Dream* and *The Tempest* (Bibliography, section 8). On the sources of the life-is-a-dream fable (Middle Eastern in origin), see Thomas 1910; Farinelli 1916; Olmedo 1928; Frenzel 1970; Richthofen 1970; Galmés de Fuentes 1986 (Bibliography, section 8).

49. For more detail on astrology and Catholic theology in the play, see, for example, Carrera Artau 1927; Febrer 1934; Lorenz 1961; Valbuena Briones 1961; May 1972; Howe 1977; Hurtado Torres 1983; De Armas 1986, 1987, 2001 (Bibliography, section 8).

50. The essence of the polemical debate over the rebel soldier can be gleaned from the initial dialogue between Hall 1968, who maintains that Sigismund's punishment of the soldier is unjust; Parker 1969, who defends the punishment as an example of poetic justice; and Hall 1969, who reaffirms his original stance (Bibliography, section 8). More or less in line with Parker's view are Connolly 1972; Halkhoree 1972; Heiple 1973; Rull

1975; McGrady 1985; Fox 1989 (Bibliography, section 8). In opposition stand May 1970; Hesse 1977; Alcalá-Zamora 1978; Homstad 1989 (Bibliography, section 8).

    51. For detailed studies of the hippogriff, see Valbuena Briones 1962; Maurin 1967; Cilveti 1973; León 1983; De Armas 1990 (Bibliography, section 8).

Translator's Notes

Rendering Calderón's *La vida es sueño* into English presents the translator with a series of difficult but unavoidable questions. Which dialect is desirable? Should archaisms be modernized or rendered into analogous English structures? Which is the most appropriate medium, verse or prose? What constitutes a scene change? How should proper names be handled? What about wordplay? And finally, what should be done with enigmatic or disputed passages? My dissatisfaction with the various answers that previous translators have given to these questions provides the primary impetus behind this new translation of the crown jewel of classical Spanish theater.

1. DIALECT

Most translators have probably spent little time consciously debating the dialect of their intended translation and have simply allowed themselves to be guided by the idiom that comes most naturally to them, that is, their native dialect. This is a reasonable principle that has guided me, too, in my rendering of Calderón into more or less standard American English. I was further motivated, however, by the fact that Calderón, although rather well-known in Britain—perhaps because of the impact of British Hispanism (especially in the wake of A. A. Parker) and the relatively high number of British translators—is still relatively unknown in the United States even at the collegiate level. Dismayed by this lacuna, comparable to leaving Sophocles or Shakespeare out of the curriculum, I have aimed primarily to produce a text that would, without sacrificing accuracy, be as accessible as possible to the current generation of American high school and college students. This choice is reflected mainly in my handling of colloquialisms. For example, Gwynne Edwards has the play's comic sidekick state in the first scene, "If only I could bloody move," whereas John Clifford, in the same scene, has him remark, "It's just someone been to the loo."[1] In contrast, I avoid terms such as *bloody* and *loo* not because they are colloquial but because their use is not widespread in American parlance. Conversely, in a different passage of the same scene, I have Bugle pronounce the more American-sounding "I'll be damned" (p. 92).

Various cultural and historical factors, of course, tend to accentuate the gap between the Spanish of Calderón and American English more than would occur, perhaps, with contemporary British English. The United States is a republic in which antiaristocratic sentiment together with veneration for democratic institutions is deeply ingrained in most citizens. Hence, notions such as the "King's English," the "royal we," or the difference between a duke and a count are likely to mean little; and I have accepted such incongruities as the inevitable price of accuracy. In the great majority of cases, however, if we discount spelling (which is, of course, not registered orally), the dialectal choices I have made are minor and likely to go almost unnoticed.

2. HISTORICITY

Languages vary not only geographically, as between Ireland, Britain, America, and Australia, but also chronologically. Standard contemporary British English is quite different from the English of Shakespeare—whose life ran roughly parallel to Calderón's (the latter was sixteen when his English contemporary died)—which is, in turn, very different from the English of Chaucer two centuries earlier. And although the evolution of the Spanish language is much less pronounced than that of English and although Castilian texts from the time of Calderón are still accessible to contemporary readers with little or no specialized training, there are some significant differences. Modern translators of Calderón are thus faced with a decision regarding not only dialect but also historicity. Whereas the former question is generally resolved with little fanfare, in accordance with the translator's native dialect, and with little consequence for reception, the second question is one that all translators must consciously face and consistently wrestle with. Its answer, furthermore, is likely to have a strong impact on the play's reception and interpretation.

Because Calderón's Spanish is roughly contemporary to the English of Shakespeare, some translators have sought to render him into an Elizabethan-sounding idiom. William Colford, for instance, translates the opening lines of the play as follows:

> Wild hippogriff, that matched the wind in flight,
> Dark lightning, dull-plumed bird, unscalèd fish,
> Brute beast that makes a mock of nature's laws,
> Now wherefore art thou come in headlong plunge
> Through twisting trails to reach this barren brink?   5
> Remain upon this crag so beasts may have
> Their Phaëthon; for I, with no more course
> Than destiny decrees, in blind despair
> Descend the tangled slope of this harsh hill
> That wrinkles to the sun its scowling brow.   10
> A poor reception, Poland, does thou give
> A stranger, since with blood her welcome's writ
> Upon thy sands, and hardly here, she fares
> So hardly. Yet my fate ordains it so.
> But where was pity e'er found for one in woe?[2]   15

Although such translations may convey an archaic feel somewhat akin to the sensation produced in a contemporary Spanish speaker upon reading Calderón in the original, the results are dubious at best because they are based upon a poor analogy. It is true that Elizabethan English was the predominant dialect in England at the time Calderón wrote *Life's a Dream,* but Colford and those who follow similar approaches are not translating the play for audiences of Elizabethan England; only a seventeenth-century translator could legitimately undertake what they have attempted.[3] If the goal of translation is to bring texts to life for audiences unable to read the original, then the translator should use the language and dialect of the audience he or she wishes to reach, realizing that readers and spectators are a product of *time* as well as space. By reconstructing a historical English dialect to translate a play from classical Spanish, Colford and others end up producing works that are no more faithful to the original than a contemporary translation would have been and that, additionally, risk alienating their potential audiences.

In contrast to such approaches, I have chosen to render Calderón into a relatively transparent, American-sounding idiom. As an example, I do not translate *tú,* the familiar form of address in both classical and contemporary Spanish, with its Elizabethan equivalent *thou* as Colford does because the latter form has since dropped out of the language and its presence throughout the play, I believe, would be jarring. At the same time, I have preserved certain anachronisms that reflect the flavor of the time without clouding the play's reception. For example, in Sigismund's first encounter with the beautiful Rossaura, he refers to his eyes as *hidrópicos,* that is, as suffering from dropsy (p. 95). Some translators paraphrase this passage so as to eliminate the reference altogether, as in Stanley Appelbaum's "my eyes must be / morbidly thirsty."[4] Yet something is lost in this move, for the belief in dropsy (today called edema) as an illness rather than a symptom says a great deal about the state of scientific knowledge in Calderón's time (see above, pp. 11–15, for more information). It is, furthermore, an unnecessary loss, for Calderón provides in the same passage enough of an explanation for audiences to grasp the basic metaphor even without specific knowledge of the condition itself.

Other lexical oddities I have preserved for similar reasons include *henbane* (p. 109) and *halberd* (p. 111) in act 2, as well as the many historical and mythological references that form such an important part of Calderón's imagery. A prime example is the famous image of the hippogriff with which the play opens. It is lamentable indeed that readers of certain translations are barred from capturing this crucial metaphor, so central to the development of the play's meaning, because the translators either dilute it through periphrasis or leave it out altogether.[5] Although not all contemporary spectators are likely to capture such allusions, one could infer the same about Calderón's peers, for even Calderón himself occasionally mixes up some of the more obscure references.[6] Yet as in the case of *dropsy,* the playwright almost always provides enough of a context in which to grasp the meaning of the reference. In the few instances where he does not—as in the allusions to Timanthes (p. 101), Lysippus (p. 101), and Atlas (p. 104)—I provide a minimal degree of clarification to orient uninformed spectators. For *readers* of my translation who desire more complete information, I provide a full explanation of such terms (which appear underlined in the text) in the Glossary, where I also include acceptable substitutions for performance, although I generally recommend against using them.

Rendering dialect and historicity is without a doubt a delicate balancing act. I can best sum up my approach by stating that my ultimate goal would be to have my readers exclaim, as Wendy Lesser does of Alfred Birnbaum's translations of Japanese novelist Haruki Murakami, "How, in short, could he make a Japanese writer sound so remarkably American without losing any of his alien allure?"[7]

3. MEDIUM: VERSE vs. PROSE

One of the more difficult questions a translator of Calderón and of classical Spanish drama in general must face is whether to imitate the plays' exclusively poetic form or, by contrast, to render into prose. If verse translations are taken to mean, minimally, line breaks that correspond more or less to those of the original, then the overwhelming preference of previous translators of Calderón (including all those written since the mid-1960s) is for verse. This choice undoubtedly reflects a sincere desire to be as faithful as possible to Calderonian form, a desire that would be betrayed—so the reasoning goes—by a prose rendition. I am convinced, however, that authentic verse translations are impossible not only practically but also theoretically because of the vast differences in the conventions of rhyme, meter, and rhythm that exist between English and Spanish poetry.

Regarding perhaps the most obvious element of poetry—rhyme—it is instructive to begin with Rossaura's widely admired opening speech, which presents a relatively simple rhyme scheme in the original Spanish, consisting of eleven pairs of rhymed *silvas* of the pattern *aA-bB-cC* . . . (where the lower case indicates verses of seven syllables and the upper case eleven). If any pattern should be imitated, it is this one because of both the simplicity of the form and the importance of the play's opening speech. Yet of the many translations to date (see section 1 of the Bibliography), only one reveals a true attempt to do so: that of the nineteenth-century Irish lawyer Denis Florence Mac-Carthy. His translation has long been out of print, but it deserves special mention for attempting such a Herculean task. Here is how Mac-Carthy renders Rossaura's opening speech:

Wild hippogriff swift speeding,
Thou that dost run, the wingèd winds exceeding,
Bolt which no flash illumes,
Fish without scales, bird without shifting plumes,
And brute awhile bereft   5
Of natural instinct, why to this wild cleft,
This labyrinth of naked rocks, dost sweep
Unreined, uncurbed, to plunge thee down the steep?
Stay in this mountain wold,
And let the beasts their Phaëton behold.   10
For I, without a guide,
Save what the laws of destiny decide,
Benighted, desperate, blind,
Take any path whatever that doth wind
Down this rough mountain to its base,   15
Whose wrinkled brow in heaven frowns in the sun's bright face.
Ah, Poland! in ill mood
Hast thou received a stranger, since in blood
The name thou writest on thy sands
Of her who hardly here fares hardly at thy hands.   20
My fate may well say so:—
But where shall one poor wretch find pity in her woe?[8]

Mac-Carthy's faithful reproduction of Calderonian rhyme, even though it briefly breaks down at various points later in the translation, is a splendid achievement that remains without peer. This particular passage, furthermore, is one of the most clearly rendered of the entire translation and thus represents a best-case scenario. Even so, the perfectly executed rhyme of Rossaura's speech comes at a high cost. The forced English syntax is at times difficult to follow, especially in an oral context. Moreover, to maintain even a semblance of the original meter, Mac-Carthy must insert meaningless words—such as "awhile" in line 5 and "benighted" in line 13—that do not exist in the original. And yet, even with such efforts, the meter runs off course as in the impossibly wordy line 16.

Mac-Carthy's technique may seem extreme, but is there any other logical approach to translating rhyme? If one aims to reproduce a given structure, shouldn't one do so consistently and in a manner that corresponds to the original, as he did? A tall order, no doubt, further complicated by the fact that the conventions of rhyme are quite different in Spanish and English. Spanish, for example, permits an assonant form of end rhyme, in which only the vowels coincide (as occurs in verses 600–1223, 1724–2017, 2188–2427, and 3094–3315 of *Life's a Dream*). How is one to translate a structure that has no real equivalent in English? In such cases even Mac-Carthy gives up and renders into free blank verse.

Faced with such difficulties, verse translators have two choices with respect to rhyme. First, they can settle for something like Edwards's nebulous approach: "a judicious mixture of end and internal rhymes, used in a way which does not distort syntax and rhythm."[9] This is, in fact, the approach most verse translators have adopted even though they may not describe it in those terms. Unfortunately, it cannot come close to reproducing Calderonian rhyme. To make matters worse, Edwards and others tend to concentrate their rhymes in the mouth of the clownish Bugle, a move that creates the lamentable and incorrect impression that rhyme in Calderón is associated with foolishness and frivolity. The second approach, which has been employed by Appelbaum on the one hand and Raine and Nadal on the other, is to jettison rhyme altogether. But such a move only brings them, despite themselves, one step closer to prose.

The second formal element of poetry—meter—is equally problematic for translators of Calderón who insist on verse renditions. The metrical system of Spanish poetry is syllabic, in which the basic unit is the syllable; and the overwhelming majority of the 3,319 verses of *Life's a Dream* consist of seven, eight, or eleven *metrical* syllables.[10] As in the case of rhyme, it seems only logical for verse translators to imitate as closely as possible the metrical structure of the play. Yet here is where, even more than with rhyme, the practical impossibility of the task is compounded by a theoretical consideration. With few exceptions, traditional English verse since the time of Chaucer has been of the accentual-syllabic variety, in which the basic unit is not the syllable but the foot, that is, a group of syllables with a defined stress pattern of varying length.[11] Although syllabic meter has been occasionally employed in English verse, it is considered experimental, the province of poets such as Auden, Pound, and Dylan Thomas; it is thus not the most appropriate choice for translating Calderón's more traditional metrical forms. What, then, would be the English metrical equivalent of a traditional eight-syllable Spanish verse, for instance? A rhetorical question, obviously, the force of which is lost on translators who insist on "a syllabic line patterned on the octosyllabic *romance.*"[12] Such methods ignore not only the fundamental metrical difference between traditional English and Spanish poetry but also the fact that, as mentioned earlier, the meter of *Life's a Dream* is not only octosyllabic but also includes a substantial number of heptasyllabic and hendacasyllabic verses.

The problem is only compounded by the third formal element of poetry—rhythm. In the words of the great French modernist poet Stéphane Mallarmé, poetry is human language "ramené à son rythme essentiel" (restored to its essential rhythm).[13] Rhythm is the most defining feature of poetry, whether classical or contemporary. This observation is easily confirmed in the Spanish poetry of Calderón's time. For example, the typical eleven-syllable verse, obligatory in sonnets and *silvas* (the latter a staple of *Life's a Dream*), presents a fixed accent on the tenth syllable and hovering accents that tend to converge over the fourth, sixth, and eighth or some combination thereof. The effect varies greatly depending on the particular combination of stressed syllables, which can be used to emphasize certain words or, alternatively, to create very peculiar, offbeat verses. In a brilliant book-length analysis, the contemporary Spanish poet Dámaso Alonso shows how well Spanish poets of the sixteenth and seventeenth centuries exploited the natural rhythm of their language in all its complexity, with profound consequences for the meaning and interpretation of their poems. Alonso's concluding remarks on Garcilaso de la Vega (1501–1536), Spain's most admired Renaissance poet, illustrate the idea:

> We have seen how the exquisite sensibility of Garcilaso uses all the expressive possibilities of rhythm as an agitator to awaken the word on the page. We have seen how this word, effectively swept away in a creative trance, thrusts itself into sudden movements and strange affinities that do not affect it, or do so only minimally, in everyday language. With what skill the rhythmic accents come to fall over exactly those words of greatest conceptual or affective expressiveness! Words enhance their aesthetic representation upon receiving the powerful light of the accent. Yes: the word, beneath the push of the accent, sometimes reinforces itself but, more frequently, as if sensually, absorbs new meaning and, increasing its phonetic expressiveness, that is, mysteriously motivating in itself the link between signifier and signified, grows in strength, richness, or color.[14]

The shadow cast by Garcilaso de la Vega was enormous: in one way or another, all subsequent Spanish poets up through the time of Calderón were indebted to him. As a consequence, any attempts at verse translations of classical Spanish poetry (whether lyric or dramatic) that do not take seriously the centrality of rhythm would seem to be missing the proverbial forest for the trees.

Rhythm is not unique to poetry, however. On the contrary, it is among the first elements that human infants process and one of the last that second-language learners master. It is, in short, one of the most deep-seated and defining features of language. The fact that the basic unit of English poetry is the foot and that of Spanish is the syllable is, in effect, a result of the great difference between the natural rhythms of the two languages. The importance of this concept for translation theory, together with the fact that few translators of Calderón seem to have given it much consideration, justifies the length of the following citation:

> Languages tend to sort out into two main rhythmic types. One type, called *syllable-timed,* has a rhythm ticked off by even syllables, each syllable receiving one quick beat called a *mora.* The general acoustic effect is a distinctive staccato "dot-dot-dot-dot-dot." The other type, *stress-timed,* has a rhythm based on stress groups. Syllables are organized into feet, each foot containing one strongly stressed syllable plus unstressed and lesser stressed satellites. Instead of each syllable taking one mora, each foot occupies about the same measure of time regardless of its number of syllables, and to equalize the feet requires that the unstressed syllables be shortened and squeezed in around the stressed ones. This yields a strikingly galloping effect, "di DUM di di DUM di DUM."
>
> English, like other Germanic languages, is stress-timed; Spanish, like most other Romance languages, is syllable-timed. Native speakers hear the difference, though they may not be able to identify precisely what is happening. Spanish strikes the English speaker as fast and machine gun–like; English, to the Spanish speaker, can seem jerky, with alternate drawling and obliteration of syllables.[15]

More recent linguistic studies, although questioning the universality of this opposition, nevertheless confirm that English and Spanish fall on opposite sides of any continuum that contrasts syllable timing and stress timing.[16] This seemingly simple difference has, in fact, radical implications that effectively sabotage from the outset any attempt to carry into English the great rhythmic richness of classical Spanish verse as studied by Dámaso Alonso. When combined with the differences already noted regarding rhyme and meter in Spanish and English, those involving rhythm seem to suggest that translators who insist on verse renderings either do not understand or simply refuse to admit the impossibility of the task they set for themselves; and although they may end up producing very beautiful-sounding translations, they cannot possibly reproduce the original form with any degree of faithfulness or consistency.[17]

Additionally, verse translations are problematic because the great lengths to which their authors are forced to go in order to accomplish what little formal similarities they manage to achieve exact a heavy toll on the content of their translations. When a translator willingly ties his hands with the clumsy constraints of rhyme, meter, and rhythm, it becomes impossible to reproduce the meaning of the text to any degree of faithfulness. When Edwards, for example, has Bugle (whom he calls Clarion) quip to the royal servant in act 2, "In other words, old friend, old cock, / The prince means put a sock in it!"[18] the imperfect end-rhyme *cock / sock in it* is accomplished only through a gross distortion of the original "Dice el príncipe muy bien, / y vos hicistes muy mal" (The prince is right, and you've acted very wrongly) (vv. 1328–1329; p. 114). Such examples abound in the many verse renderings of *Life's a Dream*. Unfortunately, in their well-intentioned attempts to reproduce both form and content, verse translators end up achieving neither—in the first case because it is impossible, in the latter because the obsession with form inevitably brings about a distortion of meaning.

My solution is to abandon form altogether in a quest for as accurate and accessible a meaning as possible. I believe the dramatic theory of Calderón's day actually supports my approach. In his humorous manifesto *The New Art of Writing Plays in This Age* (see above, p. 16, for discussion), Calderón's predecessor Lope de Vega spends over half the 390 total verses of the treatise explaining how to pick a topic, turn it into a riveting plot, and distribute the tension across the three acts of classical Spanish drama's conventional structure. He spends only six lines[19] on the differing verse forms available, which he tellingly prefaces with the caveat that "[v]erse forms should be prudently accommodated to the subjects that they describe."[20] In other words, de Vega's manifesto establishes a clear hierarchy that privileges plot and characterization (that is, content) over the more formal elements of poetry like rhyme, meter, and rhythm. Recognizing the impossibility of reproducing both form and content in the same translation, I have aimed to preserve as strictly as possible the favored term in de Vega's hierarchy, confident that doing so will convey the exceptional beauty of Calderón's poetic imagery and mitigate to some extent the loss of poetic form.

4. SCENE BOUNDARIES

One point on which both translations and Spanish-language editions of classical Spanish drama differ widely is the interpretation and placement of scene boundaries. Although the playwrights almost always indicated the divisions between the play's three main acts (called *actos* or *jornadas*), they never indicated scene divisions as do modern dramatists, that is, with the labels Scene 1, Scene 2, and so on. Calderón is no exception to this rule, and several translators of *Life's a Dream,* following his cue, also decline to mark explicit scene boundaries.[21] Two questions arise from this practice. First, is it useful to introduce into the translation a nomenclature that is absent in the original? If the answer is yes, then what method should be used to measure scenes and mark their boundaries?

In the English-speaking world, it is standard practice to divide the main acts of plays into scenes. If the playwright does not do so, editors often will. This is the case in Shakespeare, where scene divisions—not consistently indicated in the earliest available versions of his plays—were inserted by later editors, often amid disagreement.[22] Basic scene division is important for modern directors because it offers a rough index to the complexity of the performance: the more scenes there are, the more scene changes (and thus equipment necessary to produce them) will be necessary. Marking scene boundaries also provides a helpful cue to the contemporary reader of drama, often unaccustomed to visualizing the mechanics of performance. Additionally, it serves as a convenient point of reference for class discussion. It seems logical then, in translating a play for English-speaking readers, to follow the conventions with which they would be most familiar.

The question of how to mark scene boundaries is more complicated and depends on the definition of "scene" that one has in mind. The *Diccionario de Autoridades,* the first dictionary of the Royal Academy of the Spanish Language (published in the early eighteenth century and based on citations from the "authorities," that is, writers from the time of Calderón), gives two definitions of *escena*:

1. Location or place where playwrights perform their works, commonly called the Stage or the boards. Taken from the Greek *Scena,* which means a military tent or barracks, or a cover constructed from the branches of trees to offer shelter in the open field; by virtue of this [etymology], the Scene includes or signifies the place or stage with all the decorations, stage machinery, and set changes necessary for the execution of the play that is being performed.

2. A unit of the play that lasts the entire time that there are people on the stage; and thus when the stage is completely emptied and other characters enter again, it is said that another Scene begins.

The first definition, which basically means "stage," is a spatial one that implies the idea of a set; the second, which suggests that scene changes were determined by the movements of characters, is sequential or temporally based. Ideally, the two definitions coincided and reinforced one another: when all actors exited the stage, audiences imagined a *place* or *scene change* even when the meager stagecraft of Calderón's period did not make a *set change* feasible.

The academy's definitions, however, were not always completely borne out by the highly irregular theatrical practice of Spanish playwrights in the early modern period. A Latin source from Calderón's time notes that Spanish audiences "considered changes of scene superfluous, as neither the exactness of the thought, nor the elegance of the diction, nor the splendor of the production, depended upon them."[23] Another historian of Spanish theater adds: "In the public theatre in the time of Lope and Calderón scene divisions were unknown, and on the big platform stage on which these plays were p;erformed one scene flowed naturally into another without break in the action, or visible change. Only in the court theatre was scene change important, and here it is indicated by the relevant texts in their own way."[24] Sometimes a scene change could be implied by an actor's exit on the opposite side of the stage from which he entered or, alternatively, by reentry through a different door than that through which the exit was made.[25] In other instances no exit was required, and the scene change was simply implied in the dialogue or in the unveiling of one of the nine niches that formed the backdrop of the stage (see Introduction, pp. 18–19). In Lope de Vega's *The Wiles of Favia* (*Los embustes de Fabia,* c. 1590), for example, the playwright—always eager to poke fun at dramatic convention—has his character Aurelio state, without exiting the stage during a scene that takes place in his mistress's bedroom: "Here is the palace and there Nero, our Emperor, appears, for the poet has permitted this expedient to be employed, since, if the Emperor should not enter now, the narrative would be so vague that nobody would understand it."[26]

Given the confusion regarding scene divisions, nineteenth-century Spanish editors began to mark scenes whenever there was *any* new entry or exit by a character. Juan Eugenio Hartzenbusch, a founder of the classic *Library of Spanish Authors* (*Biblioteca de Autores Españoles,* 1846–1970), writes in the Introduction to a volume on Tirso de Molina:

To remind the reader, upon each entry or exit of a speaking character, the names of those who were speaking before he entered or who continue to speak after he exits, is good for the memory, facilitates the understanding of the drama, gives beauty to the book as well as a rest and a break to the eyes of he who reads; thus, following the example offered by the *Standard Collection of Selected Plays* (*Colección general de Comedias escogidas*), which began publication in the year 1826, we have subdivided the dramas of Tirso into scenes.[27]

The practice of measuring scenes by the entrances and exits of characters, which may have its origin in eighteenth-France,[28] was defended by Wolfgang Kayser in twentieth-century Germany on the grounds that it is useful for directors to know that each scene will have a fixed number of actors.[29] Perhaps resting on the authority of people like Kayser and Hartzenbusch (who was an accomplished playwright as well as an editor), many modern editors of the Spanish Comedia still follow a similar practice. In the Cátedra edition of *La vida es sueño,* for instance, Ciriaco Morón Arroyo indicates eight scenes in act 1, nineteen in act 2, and fourteen in act 3 even though each act has only two or three settings.[30] Several of the play's English-language translators reckon scenes in the same way.[31]

Although Kayser may be right that it is helpful to directors to have the play's basic units associated with a fixed number of actors, it is equally helpful, in questions of setting and staging, to see the play broken down into unities of place—a perspective not possible in his scheme. Moreover, Kayser's approach may mislead or disorient general readers more accustomed to English-language conventions. Finally, it is not followed by contemporary Spanish playwrights.

It does not seem justified, then, to imitate a practice that is employed in neither the English-speaking world nor the contemporary Spanish-speaking world and, at best, only inconsistently in classical Spanish theater. Some editors thus suggest a different approach, as J. E. Varey explains:

> Evidently, an act is usually conceived by the dramatist as divided into sections, which [Geoffrey] Ribbans has suggested should be called *cuadros,* a word less evocative of "scenery" than *escena.* A *cuadro* ends when all the characters leave the stage, and another set of characters appear, thus indicating to the audience a change of location, also indicated to the audience by direct textual references, by the costumes worn by the actors, and by their method of acting.[32]

Varey's suggestion, which has been endorsed by others,[33] streamlines the unwieldy approach of nineteenth-century editors; at the same time, it remains remarkably close to the eighteenth-century academy's definition of *escena*. Because I attempt to strike a balance in my own translation between the requirements of modern readers and faithfulness to the original, I find this method entirely satisfactory and have employed it in my version of the play, using the word *scene* given that there is no other acceptable translation of *cuadro* (which means, in the first instance, *picture* or *painting*).[34]

5. PROPER NAMES

Calderón almost certainly took some of the character names in *Life's a Dream* from a tedious and little-known Byzantine novel, *Eustorgio and Clorilene, A Muscovite Tale* (*Eustorgio y Clorilene, historia moscovica*), published in 1629 by Enrique Suárez de Mendoza y Figueroa.[35] Others may have been inspired by his readings in history and mythology or were simply the result of pure invention or fancy. The handling of this diverse gallery of names is another point on which translators diverge rather broadly. Most have opted for a limited approach, selectively translating certain names while leaving others as is. Following is a summary of all character names from the play that have been rendered into English (translators are listed in parentheses).

Astolfo: Astolof (Mandel)

Astrea: Astraea (Appelbaum, Birch and Trend, Mitchell and Barton, Oxenford)

Basilio: Basil (Campbell, Stirling), Basilius (Mac-Carthy), Bazylic (Mandel), King (Trench)

Clarín: Bocazas (Williamson), Clarion (Birch and Trend, Campbell, Edwards, Mitchell and Barton, Stirling), Fife (FitzGerald), Piper (Raine and Nadal)

Clorilene: Chlorylene (Stirling), Clorilena (Oxenford), Clorileña (FitzGerald)

Estrella: Stella (Campbell)

Eustorgio: Alfonso (FitzGerald), Eustorgius (Campbell, Mac-Carthy, Edwards, Stirling)

Recisunda: Recsunde (Stirling), Rosamunda (Mac-Carthy), Ruscinda (Edwards)

Rosaura: Rosanka (Mandel)

Segismundo: Segismund (Campbell, FitzGerald), Sigismund (Birch and Trend, Mac-Carthy, Mandel, Mitchell and Barton, Oxenford, Trench), Sigmund (Stirling)

As this list makes clear, there is little rhyme or reason behind the names most frequently selected for translation or the ways in which they have been translated. Perhaps this fact explains why, in recent years, the tendency has been toward not translating any character names.[36] Yet the seeming consistency of such an approach is belied by the fact that the same translators routinely translate proper geographic names; few would think of not translating *Polonia* as *Poland,* for example.[37] But if geographic names are to be translated, why not character names?

The simple answer is that preexisting, standardized translations exist for most major geographic names: Italy for Italia, Pyrenees for Pirineos, Thames for Támesis, and so on. Although this is also the case with many common personal names, especially those with a Latin or Greek root, others have no standard translation. But to translate only those names that have an obvious counterpart in the other language is to erect a boundary between the domestic and the alien that does not necessarily exist in the original. Some personal names, furthermore, have special meanings in Spanish that often serve as the basis for wordplay; if left untranslated, those meanings are bound to be lost on an English-speaking audience.

At a bare minimum, I have sought to achieve the consistency lacking in my predecessors by translating or reinventing all character names of the original. I have aimed to produce names that are faithful to the spirit of Calderón's play but that also facilitate pronunciation by monolingual actors as well as comprehension by monolingual audiences. These goals required different approaches depending on the name. With those that seem to allude to historical figures, I have employed the most suggestive English equivalents. Sometimes a literal or close to literal translation was called for, as in the case of *Bugle* or *Stella.* Other names are no doubt intended to bear a foreign or exotic feel, even in Spanish, in which case an obvious translation does not immediately suggest itself. In such cases I have attempted to preserve the name's alien quality while still adapting the roots of the original to a more intuitively English phonetic system.

Detailed explanations of each name follow; when necessary, pronunciation keys are offered in brackets at the end of the entry. Directors, of course, should feel free to restore the originals (provided in parentheses) for the purpose of performance, but they should realize that in doing so, many of the puns made possible by such translations as *Bugle* for *Clarín* and *Stella* for *Estrella* (see below, pp. 62 and 64, for example) will be lost.

Aistulf (Astolfo)—Originally the name of an eighth-century Lombard king (Aistulf of Friuli) who threatened the Papal States and was defeated by Pepin the Short (Charlemagne's father) in 754 and again in 756. Also a character in Ariosto's *Orlando furioso* (based on the legends of Charlemagne), where he is cousin to the hero Orlando. The latter source may have led Calderón to the historical figure. If this is the case, he may have chosen the name as an allusion to the duke's naked grab for power and a foreshadowing of his ultimate defeat by Sigismund. Balachov 1969 and Ziomek 1975 associate Aistulf with Wladislaus IV, son of Sigismund III and king of Poland from 1595 to 1648, but Strzalko 1959 and Baczynska 1991 link Wladislaus to Sigismund (Bibliography, section 8). [ACE-tulf]

Astraea (Astrea)—An archaic Greek divinity who coexisted on earth with mortals during the Golden Age, fostering justice and virtue; when the Golden Age degenerated, she fled and was eventually transformed into the constellation Virgo. The astral connotations of her name link her to Stella, whom she (that is, Rossaura in disguise) serves as lady-in-waiting. [Uh-STRAY-uh]

Bugle (Clarín)—A direct translation. Sidekicks in early modern Spanish theater often had comic-sounding names indicative of a particular vice or other character flaw (in Bugle's case, his inability to keep his mouth shut). The name is subject to various puns throughout the play.

Clorilyn (Clorilene)—Curiously named both as Vasily's older sister (and Stella's mother) in Aistulf's first encounter with Stella and as Vasily's wife in the king's long confessional soliloquy at court (for a discussion of this coincidence, see above, pp. 31–32, and below, pp. 65–66). She is one of the protagonists of Mendoza's novel, albeit in a very different role (Eustorgio's beloved). [KLOR-ih-lin]

Clothold (Clotaldo)—Perhaps suggestive of the Greek fate Clotho, who spun the web of life that animated souls (Molho 1993, p. 250 [Bibliography, section 8]). As Sigismund's only contact with the outside world, Clothold has control over the prince's life in a similar fashion. Additionally, he is Rossaura's biological father as well as her protector, leading her to proclaim him her life-giver on several occasions. Ziomek 1983 (Bibliography, section 8) relates the character to the Polish minister Jan Zamoyski. [KLOW-thuld]

Eustorge (Eustorgio)—From the Greek *eu* (good) + *storge* (familial love), an etymology that offers an ironic contrast to the estranged relationship between Vasily and Sigismund. Eustorgio is the protagonist of Mendoza's novel, where he is the son of Basilio and the lover of Clorilene. [YOU-storj]

Grethissunda (Recisunda)—A strange name probably invented for its exotic feel, perhaps on analogy with Segismundo. [Greh-thi-SOON-duh]

Rossaura (Rosaura)—A name apparently formed by a combination of *Rosa* (rose) and *Aura* (breeze), perhaps suggesting the character's beauty as well as her restlessness. *Aura* also recalls the Latin *aurum* (gold), possibly indicating Rossaura's inner worth. Molho 1993 (pp. 238–239; Bibliography, section 8) associates the name with the figure of the bear. [Ruh-SOAR-uh. The *s*-sound should be pronounced as in *Jessica*.]

Sigismund (Segismundo)—Another name that Calderón probably came across in his readings of history, as several European monarchs bore it including three Polish kings in the sixteenth and seventeenth centuries (see the entries that follow, adapted from the *Columbia Encyclopedia* 2002 [Bibliography, section 5]). Molho 1993 (227–229; Bibliography, section 8) associates the name with the figure of the wolf. The more familiar, syncopated form of the name is Sigmund. Both versions are Germanic in origin and mean "protector [*mund*] of victories [*sige*]," although it is unlikely that Calderón would have been aware of the etymology. [SIG-is-mund. The *g*-sound should be pronounced as in girl.]

Sigismund I—1467–1548, son of Casimir IV, ruled Poland from 1506 to 1548. Elected to succeed his brother, Alexander I, Sigismund faced the problem of consolidating his domestic power to counter external threats to Poland. The enactment during Alexander's rule of the law Nihil Novi (1505), which forbade kings to enact laws without the consent of the Diet, seriously handicapped Sigismund in his struggle with the magnates and nobles. Nevertheless, in 1527 he established a regular army and a fiscal system to finance its maintenance. Intermittent war with Vasily III of Moscow began in 1507; in 1514 Smolensk fell to the Muscovite forces. In 1515 Sigismund entered an alliance with Holy Roman Emperor Maximilian I. Maximilian acknowledged the provisions of the Second Peace of Toru, and Sigismund consented to the marriage of the children of his brother, Wladislaus II of Bohemia and Hungary, to Maximilian's grandchildren. Through this double marriage contract Bohemia and Hungary passed to the house of Hapsburg when Sigismund's nephew Louis II died in 1526. Sigismund's wars against the Teutonic knights ended in 1525, when their grand master, Albert of Brandenburg—having converted to Lutheranism—secularized the order and did homage to Sigismund, who invested him with the domains of the order as the first duke of Prussia. Sigismund sought peaceful relations with the khans of Crimea but was still involved in border warfare with them. Sigismund was a humanist; he and his second wife, Bona Sforza, daughter of Gian Galeazzo Sforza of Milan, were patrons of Renaissance culture, which began to flower in Poland during their reign.

Sigismund II—1520–1572, also known as Sigismund Augustus, ruled Poland from 1548 to 1572. Crowned in 1530 to assure his succession, he assumed the royal functions upon the death of his father, Sigismund I. By the Union of Lublin in 1569, he transferred his hereditary grand duchy of Lithuania to the Polish crown, creating the unified Polish-Lithuanian state. His great diplomatic skill enabled him to conciliate the dissident elements both in Poland and among the Lithuanian magnates who opposed the fusion. Upon the dissolution of the Livonian Brothers of the Sword in 1561, Sigismund gained control over Courland, Latgale, and other parts of Livonia. Opposed in this claim by Holy Roman Emperor Ferdinand I, in 1562 Sigismund granted the elector of Brandenburg hereditary succession in the duchy of Prussia in exchange for diplomatic support. The widened frontiers brought Sigismund into conflict with Ivan IV of Russia, who took Polotsk in 1563. The Polish Reformation reached its height during Sigismund's reign; in 1570 most Protestant sects formed a union to strengthen their cause. An open-minded, tolerant monarch and a loyal Roman Catholic, Sigismund sought to counteract the Reformation peacefully; he abolished the ecclesiastic courts in 1562 but introduced the Society of Jesus in 1565, which successfully preached the Counter Reformation. The Renaissance flowered at this time, and Sigismund was an

accomplished humanist and theologian. The last of the Jagiello dynasty
to rule Poland, Sigismund died childless.

Sigismund III—1566–1632, king of Poland 1587–1632 and of Sweden
1592–1599. The son of John III of Sweden and Catherine, sister of
Sigismund II of Poland, he united the Vasa and Jagiello dynasties. He
was a Roman Catholic, and his marriage to Anne of Hapsburg in 1592
linked him to the Catholic monarchs of Europe. A period of factional
strife after the death of King Stephen Báthory in 1586 was ended by
the election of Sigismund as king of Poland. In 1592 Sigismund inher-
ited the Swedish throne from his father, but his reluctance to accept
Protestantism as the state religion in Sweden involved him in conflict
with the Swedes and with his uncle, who was regent. Although officially coronated in 1594, Sigismund was defeated at Stangebro in 1598
and was formally deposed by the Swedish Diet in 1599. He retained
his claims to Sweden and after 1600 fought intermittently with his
uncle and later with his nephew, Gustavus II, to whom he lost most of
Livonia in 1629. Sigismund dreamed of conquering all of Russia, and
in 1610, taking advantage of the chaos there after the death of Boris
Godunov, he continued his military campaign and took Moscow. In
1612 an improvised Russian army under Prince Pozharski expelled the
Poles, who retained Smolensk and other border towns. Peace with
Russia (1634) came only after Sigismund's death. Sigismund's pro-
Catholic policy helped to effect the union in 1596 of the Ruthenian
Church in Poland-Lithuania with the Church of Rome. Sigismund's
rule also saw the start of intermittent war with the Ottoman Empire,
lasting until Poland obtained a favorable treaty in 1621. Sigismund's
use of Austrian aid to limit the powers of the Diet and the dissatisfaction of the Protestants led to a rebellion in 1606–1607 under Nicholas
Zebrzydowski, the palatine of Krakow. Although the rebels were defeated, their cause triumphed, and no more attempts were made to
change the constitution.

Stella (Estrella)—Literally *star,* although much more prevalent as a name in
Spanish than *Star* is in English. I have chosen the Latin form because its
frequency in English is similar to that of *Estrella* in Spanish while still allow-
ing the various puns to which the name gives rise throughout the play.

Vasily (Basilio)—A name that seems to be the result of an extraordinary set of coincidences. First, it is derived from the Greek *basileus,* meaning simply "king," suggesting the archetypal nature of Vasily's character. Second, it is one of the proper names in Mendoza's novel, where Basilio is the father (rather than the son) of Eustorgio. Third, it was the name of several early modern Muscovite princes, one of whom, Vasily III, went to war with Sigismund I of Poland (see entry under Sigismund); Ginard de la Rosa 1881 (pp. 296–297; Bibliography, section 8) suggests that Calderón could have learned these names through the Polish and Russian ambassadors at the Spanish court. I have adopted the Slavic spelling (elided in Spanish) to give the name a flavor consistent with the play's setting. [Vuh-SIL-ee. The *s*-sound should be pronounced as in *Rossaura.*]

Viola (Violante)—A name that suggests both *violet* and the *violation* of Clothold's secret wedding vow to this character. [Vie-OH-luh]

6. WORDPLAY

Wordplay, a defining feature of the language of *Life's a Dream* and of the Spanish Baroque in general (see Introduction, p. 7), bridges many typological divides. Some instances are produced for comic effect; others enhance the gravity of the situation. Some are unintentional on the part of the characters; others are quite deliberate. Some arise from a likeness in form, whereas others are based on similar meanings or concepts. Finally, all characters engage in the phenomenon, from the most humble to the most noble. Consequently, any translation that does not make a serious effort to transmit wordplay cannot but undermine the play's original meaning and flavor. Unfortunately, many previous translators have either suppressed certain instances of wordplay (perhaps because they were unaware of them; perhaps because they considered them inappropriate, insignificant, or impossible to capture in verse) or rendered them so clumsily as to be meaningless. In my translation I have taken care to render wordplay as closely as possible to the meaning and register of the original. My aim has been to transmit the playfulness of the Spanish in a way that can be apprehended in a performance context (where a translated pun requiring a footnote to explain it cannot be considered successful).

For readers with a working knowledge of Spanish, I have included the following commentaries on some of the more significant cases of wordplay, referenced by the verse numbers of the original and followed by my renderings and the page numbers on which they appear. The words in play are underlined.

Y apenas llega cuando llega a penas (v. 20); "and hardly is he come when he comes into hardship" (p. 91). The first and most famous pun in the play enhances the gravity of Rossaura's desperate circumstances.

[Ros.] Tus pies beso / mil veces. [Bug.] Y yo los viso, / que una letra más o menos / no reparan los amigos (vv. 894–897); "I shall adorn your feet a thousand times with my kisses.—I'll just adore them from afar, for what's a letter or two between friends?" (p. 105). Given that Spanish *b* and *v* are pronounced identically (at the beginning of a word, much like English *b*), only the *e*- and *i*-sounds differentiate the two words in play, which, of course, have very different meanings—one indicating reverence, the other distance. Bugle invokes the slight phonetic difference to excuse his comical lack of respect.

Despojado y despejado / se asoma a su desvergüenza (vv. 1176–77); "a shallow pocket can be overcome with a deep wit and an insolent attitude" (p. 111). This pun, the culmination of one of the play's more opaque passages, is also among the most difficult to translate not only because of the linguistic play but also because the context that would have made it intelligible to spectators of Calderón's time is rather far removed from contemporary America. Bugle has just explained how he has fought his way into the palace to follow the drama in which Prince Sigismund has been swept away. The metaphor is based on the language of public spectacle, where those who, like Bugle, are penniless (*despojado*) must be quick-witted and alert (*despejado*) to gain a good view; if they are, they can rely on their own insolence (*desvergüenza*) to create something like a box seat for them.

[Sig.] Tú sólo en tan nuevos mundos / me has agradado. [Bug.] Señor, / soy un grande agradador / de todos los Segismundos (vv. 1336–39); "You're the only one in this princely world I find entertaining.—My lord, I'm a great entertainer of all worldly princes" (p. 115). A simple pun based on the similarity of Sigismund's Spanish name (*Segismundo*) with the word for world (*mundo*).

[Serv. 2] Es grande. [Sig.] Mayor soy yo (v. 1371); "He's titled.—I'm more entitled!" (p. 115). One of the more meaningful instances of wordplay in the play. The upper echelons of Spanish nobility, called *grandes,* were granted the unique privilege of wearing their hats in the king's presence; thus the servant is attempting to defend the duke's behavior to the prince. Unschooled in courtly

etiquette, Sigismund misunderstands the servant's comment and interprets *grande* in the wider sense of "great"; his response means, literally, "I'm greater." Most translators emphasize this second meaning of the word—the one on which Sigismund focuses—but in doing so they elide the first meaning (i.e., a rank of nobility) and thus neutralize the double entendre on which the wordplay is based.

Aunque el <u>parabién</u> es <u>bien</u> / darme del <u>bien</u> que conquisto, / sólo de haberos hoy visto / os admito el <u>parabién</u>; / y así, del llegarme a ver / con el <u>bien</u> que no merezco, / el <u>parabién</u> agradezco (vv. 1392–98); "Although it were <u>well</u> to wish me <u>well</u> on the <u>wealth</u> that I inherit, I deserve more <u>well-wishing</u> just for having seen you today; and thus, I appreciate your <u>well-wishing</u> for finding myself before such unmerited <u>wealth</u>" (p. 116). A veritable orgy of internal and end rhyme, this instance of wordplay is meant to imitate (and perhaps to parody) the flowery language characteristic of courtly interaction. The play stems, on the one hand, from the lexical similarity between *parabién* (congratulations) and *bien* and, on the other, from the double grammatical function of the latter as an adverb meaning "well" and a noun meaning "good," "goodness," or "wealth."

Nada me parece <u>justo</u> / en siendo contra mi <u>gusto</u> (vv. 1417–18); "Nothing is <u>right</u> when it contradicts my <u>delight</u>" (p. 116). Although the play on *justo* (just, right) and *gusto* (delight, pleasure) is technically just a simple rhyme, I have decided, contrary to my normal procedure, to translate it as a rhyme because of the prominence it is accorded in Spanish literature of Calderón's time. Its popularity can perhaps be explained by the fact that it neatly encapsulates the tension that gave rise to so many dramatic plots, pitting the desire of the individual against the collective will of society.

. . . mi <u>primo</u> Astolfo—bastara / que mi <u>primo</u> te dijese (vv. 1794–95); " . . . my <u>first cousin</u> Aistulf—it should be enough to say he's my <u>first</u>" (p. 125). A pun that plays on the various meanings of *primo*: "cousin," "peer" (of the king), "spouse" (in noble marriages), and "first."

[Bug.] ¿A qué fin / me encierran? [Clo.] Eres <u>Clarín</u>. / [Bug.] Pues ya digo que seré / <u>corneta</u>, y que callaré, / que es instrumento ruin (vv. 2043–47); "What's your purpose in locking me up?—You're <u>Bugle</u>.—Well, I'll call myself <u>Horn</u> from now on, and I'll keep quiet as befits those with horns" (p. 129). One of the many examples of wordplay involving Bugle's name in Spanish (Clarín), which is lost if the name goes untranslated. In this case the pun's literal meaning derives from a comparison between the virile bugle, an instrument associated

with war, and the more refined cornet; the figurative meaning plays on the association between the Spanish *corneta* and the figure of the cuckold (*cornudo*), who was frequently described as wearing horns and was best served by remaining silent about his wife's infidelity.

En el filósofo leo / <u>Nicomedes</u>, y las noches / en el concilio <u>Niceno</u> (vv. 2217–19); "I find myself in a prison where the <u>board is bare</u> and the <u>menu mean</u>" (p. 133). Rivaling the *despojado/despejado* opposition in the quest for obscurity, this pun comes in a scene in which Bugle is explaining the treatment he has received since being imprisoned at the end of act 2. High on his list of complaints is the lack of food, which gives rise to the wordplay. Bugle explains that, having nothing else to do, he reads the "philosopher" Nicomedes by day and the teachings of the Nicene Council by night. Because both proper names are historically based, it seems plausible that they might have registered with readers of Calderón's day, and that minimal degree of plausibility is all that is necessary to facilitate the pun. Yet in truth, none of the individuals named Nicomedes left any known writings, whereas the canons of the two Nicene Councils would probably have struck Calderón's contemporaries as rather remote.[38] Furthermore, given Bugle's humble station in life, it is doubtful that he would have been able to read. This is a case, in fact, where the words are simply shells with no independent meaning or relationship to each other (apart from the curious coincidence that Nicaea, the seat of the Nicene Council, was in Bithynia, home to the Nicomedes dynasty). The real import of these proper names lies in their phonetic value, which enables the double entendre. As with *apenas/a penas*, *Nicomedes* can be read as two words: *ni-comedes*, which means (in Old Spanish) "you get no lunch." Similarly, *Niceno* breaks down into *ni-ceno* or "I get no supper."

[Soldiers.] Danos tus <u>plantas</u>. [Bug.] No puedo / porque las he menester / para mí, y fuera defeto / ser príncipe <u>desplantado</u> (vv. 2249–52); "Grant us the <u>soles</u> of your feet.—I can't because I need them for myself, and I wouldn't do you much good as a <u>de-solate</u> prince" (p. 134). One of Bugle's many humorous puns, this one is based on the double meaning of *plantas*: "soles of the feet" and "plants." The soldiers use the word in the first sense to ask for Bugle's feet in order to kiss them. He responds by saying he cannot give them away because doing so would leave him *desplantado*: literally "de-soled" or "de-footed," but also "uprooted," "obliterated," or "exiled." As is the case with many of the play's puns, most translations capture only one sense of the double entendre.

Heredera de fortunas / corrí con ella una propia (vv. 2776–77); "her <u>stormy</u> <u>fortune</u> ran me through many <u>shipwrecks</u> of my own" (p. 144). Based on a play between *fortuna,* meaning "luck" or "fortune," and the expression *correr fortuna,* frequent in nautical terminology, meaning "to run into stormy weather."

¿Quién creerá que, habiendo sido / una <u>estrella</u> quien conforma / dos amantes, sea una <u>Estrella</u> / la que los divida agora (vv. 2794–97); "Who would have guessed that, having been brought together through <u>stellar design</u>, we would now be separated by <u>Stella's design</u>?" (p. 144). One of the many examples of wordplay involving Stella's name in Spanish (Estrella). The pun is lost if the name goes untranslated.

7. TEXTUAL VARIANTS AND OBSCURITIES

All surviving texts of the late medieval and early modern periods are products of a printing process in its infancy. Technology was primitive at best, and orthographic conventions varied widely. Furthermore, the more popular a book was, the more printings were made of it and the more subject it became to the fallibility of the process. The works we read today frequently do not represent any single original but rather are the fruits of a long, laborious procedure that involves collating and comparing the different versions available in an attempt to come up with an edition that most faithfully represents the author's intentions. Such is the task of textual criticism, and readers must be aware that, just as in literary criticism, the final product always represents an *interpretation.* This is especially the case with dramatic works, whose path from author to printer was especially sinuous and involved long detours through acting companies, where passages were often added, removed, or emended at will.[39]

The text that we are able to reconstruct of *Life's a Dream* comes from two main branches, both of which date back to editions published in 1636, one in Madrid (M) and the other in Zaragoza (Z). According to Ruano de la Haza, the Z-branch, which consists of eight texts, predates the M-branch (four texts) by several years, placing its origin in the late 1620s.[40] Overall, the two branches diverge on about 40 percent of the total number of verses,[41] forcing editors to make a significant decision regarding the product they ultimately present to readers. Because the basic difference seems to be that M represents a more polished, literary version whereas Z is more spontaneous and appropriate for the theater (it contains more stage directions, for example),[42] choosing one over the other is particularly difficult. One point that tips the balance toward M in my mind is that every major critical edition of the play in Spanish is based on M rather than Z; thus what people in the Spanish-speaking world know as *La vida es sueño* is, 99 percent of the time, a knowledge of M. To publish for the English-speaking world a translation of the play based on Z would create an unreasonable imbalance in popular knowledge of the play and lead to not a few misunderstandings. For instance, Z contains very little of the prince's beautiful and much-admired soliloquy on dreams that appears in M at the end of act 2 (pp. 131–132); because this is one of the passages that have made the play famous both inside and outside Spain, I find its absence in Z a strong argument in favor of M. Furthermore and perhaps more important, it is clear from Calderón's personal involvement in the Madrid edition of 1636 that M is the text he intended to bequeath to posterity.[43]

After consulting many Spanish-language editions of the play, I have used as the basis of my translation that of J. M. Ruano de la Haza (Castalia 2000). Ruano's phenomenal command of both the play's textual history and its dramatic dimensions, his scrupulous attention to detail, and his always constructive dialogue with his predecessors have resulted in a highly reliable text that renders most previous editions obsolete (along with, I would venture to add, translations based on them). Like many editors, Ruano takes M as his base, but his exceptional knowledge of Z allows him to correct many problematic passages where his predecessors have failed. It is thus an edition that represents the best possible compromise between the literary value of M and the dramatic appeal of Z.

Apart from those passages disputed by textual critics, there are a number of simply enigmatic or obscure passages in which the meaning is not always readily apparent. In many such cases Ruano's remarkable intuitions, clearly explained in his excellent notes, have proved invaluable to me. In some instances a simple stage direction can clarify an elliptical passage, and I have liberally supplemented the text in this way.[44] A different punctuation, too, can sometimes resolve an otherwise enigmatic passage.[45] Discounting stage directions and punctuation, I have diverged from Ruano's text on only five occasions.[46] I have been careful, furthermore, not to resolve ambiguities that may have been part of Calderón's design. One passage deserves particular mention in this regard. In act 1 of the play, when Aistulf recounts the royal genealogy to Stella, he explains that her mother was named Clorilyn (v. 521, p. 100). Only 140 verses later in the original, Vasily refers to his wife as Clorilyn (v. 660, p. 102). Is this an oversight on Calderón's part, or did he have something else in mind? More than half of previous translators evidently see it as an error that must be corrected, for they have either eliminated or altered one of the two references to Clorilyn.[47] I believe, in fact, that this passage may provide an important key to the play's interpretation (see above, pp. 31–32) and that at the very least it should be left to the readers or spectators to decide. As a general rule, I prefer to let stand a possible error rather than neutralize a potentially meaningful ambiguity.

IN CONCLUSION, I HOPE TO ACQUAINT a new generation of students and theatergoers with a translation of Calderón that is accurate, accessible, and— most of all—playable, for I firmly agree with the contention that drama translators must "see written text and performance as *indissolubly linked.*"[48] The major problem with previous translations of *Life's a Dream* stems from a failure to recognize that indissoluble link, resulting in a formal stiffness of language that is little conducive to oral reception. All of the decisions I have made, in one way or another, are aimed at avoiding such stiffness. As a final example, the reader will note that I have made liberal use of contractions, as evidenced in my translation of the play's title. A few previous translators have done so as well, but most have not. (Since the early 1970s, in fact, only Mitchell and Barton's adaptation has used a contraction in the title.) Although we are admonished against their use in standard written English, contractions more accurately represent the norms of the spoken language and are thus more appropriate in the oral context of theater.

There is no doubt that *Life's a Dream* stands up to the highest literary standards. I hope to have preserved its literary qualities while at the same time creating a genuine *script* for the performance of this extraordinary play.

NOTES

1. Edwards 1991, p. 105; Clifford 1998, p. 5 (Bibliography, section 1a).

2. Colford 1958, pp. 1–2 (Bibliography, section 1a).

3. Other translators who adopt an Elizabethan-sounding idiom include Oxenford 1842; Trench 1856; Mac-Carthy 1873; Stirling 1942; FitzGerald 2000 (Bibliography, sections 1a, 1b).

4. Appelbaum 2002, p. 7. Similarly, Clifford 1998 translates as "My eyes must have a kind of rabies" (p. 10), whereas Raine and Nadal 1968 render "There is a fever in my

eyes" (p. 7); Edwards 1991 translates the passage even more periphrastically: "my eyes are so / Entranced, they long to see you more, / And hunger for the sight of you, / As if they were a man to whom / Drink is forbidden" (p. 109). See Bibliography, section 1a.

5. For example: "This headstrong horse must think itself / An eagle or some fabulous beast" (Edwards 1991, p. 103); "Where have you thrown me, mad horse, / half griffin?" (Honig 1993, p. 293); and "There, four-footed / Fury, blast- /-engender'd Brute" (FitzGerald 2000, p. 376). See Bibliography, sections 1a, 1b.

6. Indeed, even some of Calderón's translators misspell *Phaëthon,* failing to restore the *h* that drops out in the passage from classical Greek to modern Spanish. See Oxenford 1842, p. 256; Mac-Carthy 1873, p. 7; Edwards 1991, p. 103; Clifford 1998, p. 3; FitzGerald 2000, p. 376 (Bibliography, sections 1a, 1b).

7. Lesser 2002, p. B5 (Bibliography, section 4).

8. Mac-Carthy 1873, pp. 7–8 (Bibliography, section 1a).

9. Edwards 1991, p. xxxi (Bibliography, section 1a).

10. One must distinguish between *metrical* and *phonetic* syllables because Spanish poets make use of certain licenses that allow for the combination, addition, or deletion of syllables for purposes of meter; when any such license is employed (which happens fairly regularly), the total number of poetic syllables will differ from the total number of actual (phonetic) syllables. For a brief summary of versification in Spanish poetry, see Rivers 1988, pp. 23–24 (Bibliography, section 3). More detailed treatment is offered in Baehr 1970 and Navarro Tomás 1991 (Bibliography, section 3).

11. See Kinzie 1999 (Bibliography, section 3), especially pp. 215–216, for more detail on the history of English prosody.

12. Honig 1993, p. x (Bibliography, section 1a).

13. Mallarmé 1965 (Bibliography, section 3).

14. Alonso 1993, p. 105 (Bibliography, section 3).

15. Whitley 1986, pp. 65–66 (Bibliography, section 4).

16. See, for example, Frota and Vigário 2001; Grabe and Ling Low 2002 (Bibliography, section 4). My thanks to Professor José Ignacio Hualde for these references.

17. See the 1989 collection of articles by Dixon, Edwards, Gitlitz, MacKenzie, McGaha, Muir, and Paterson (Bibliography, section 4), all leaders in the field of Comedia translation. With the lone exception of McGaha, all vehemently defend verse translations. Although they demonstrate an often keen awareness of some of the problems explored in this section, especially those regarding rhyme and meter, these critics tend to see the difficulty not as a theoretical impasse but rather as a practical stumbling block that can be overcome through patience and ingenuity. Significantly, none shows any knowledge of those studies in linguistics that demonstrate the great, irreconcilable differences between the natural rhythms of English and Spanish as discussed earlier.

18. Edwards 1991, p. 140 (Bibliography, section 1a).

19. Vega Carpio 1989, vv. 307–312 (Bibliography, section 3).

20. Ibid., vv. 305–306.

21. Campbell 1985; Edwards 1991; Clifford 1998; Appelbaum 2002 (Bibliography, section 1a).

22. The editors of *The Norton Shakespeare*, for example, justify their particular reckoning of scenes in *Henry the Sixth, Part One* as follows: "Generally, additional scenes are marked at all points during a battle when the stage appears momentarily to be clear of all characters, the traditional indication in the Renaissance theater that one scene has ended and another begun" (Greenblatt 1997, p. 442 [Bibliography, section 3]).

23. Quoted in Rennert 1963, p. 86n (Bibliography, section 8).

24. Shergold 1967, pp. xxiv–xxv (Bibliography, section 8).

25. Rennert 1963, pp. 87–88; Shergold 1967, p. 361 (Bibliography, section 8).

26. Quoted in Rennert 1963 (translation Rennert), p. 87 (Bibliography, section 8).

27. Hartzenbusch 1924, p. ix (Bibliography, section 8).

28. I am grateful to Michael McGaha for this insight, although I have been unable to document it.

29. Kayser 1954, pp. 268–269 (Bibliography, section 3).

30. Morón Arroyo 2000 (Bibliography, section 2).

31. Mac-Carthy 1873; Stirling 1942; Colford 1958; Raine and Nadal 1968 (Bibliography, section 1a).

32. Varey 1985a, p. 158 (Bibliography, section 8).

33. Ruano de la Haza and Allen 1994, pp. 291–294; Allen 1996 (Bibliography, section 8).

34. Other translators who follow this approach to scene divisions include Oxenford 1842; Birch and Trend 1925; Huberman and Huberman 1962; Mitchell and Barton 1990; Honig 1993; FitzGerald 2000 (Bibliography, sections 1a, 1b).

35. See Praag 1936 (Bibliography, section 8) for a summary.

36. This is the case with Colford 1958; Huberman and Huberman 1962; Honig 1993; Clifford 1998. Appelbaum 2002 maintains all the original Spanish names except Astrea, which he restores to its Latin spelling (Astraea). See Bibliography, section 1a.

37. After writing this sentence I came across Laird Williamson's adaptation (2001 [Bibliography, section 1b]), which indeed leaves *Polonia* untranslated. Nevertheless, I believe my point remains valid for serious translations.

38. Nicomedes was not a philosopher but rather the name assumed by a line of kings of ancient Bithynia from the third to the first centuries B.C.; the name also belonged to a little-known Greek mathematician of the second century B.C., but it seems unlikely, given his obscurity, that Calderón's allusion would have been made with him in mind. The first Nicene Council convened in A.D. 325 to deal with the heresy of Arianism (the denial of Christ's divinity); the second met in 787 to address the problem of iconoclasm (the movement, prominent in the Eastern Church, against the worship of images). Both issues had been long defused by Calderón's time.

39. See Varey 1985a (Bibliography, section 8) for more detail on the printing process.

40. Ruano de la Haza 2000, pp. 7–9 (Bibliography, section 2).

41. Ibid., p. 15.

42. Ibid., pp. 15–18.

43. Ibid., p. 18.

44. Notably scarce in playwrights of Calderón's time (including Shakespeare), stage directions were particularly susceptible to reduction or elimination by penny-pinching printers, and their scarcity is one of the most disorienting elements for modern readers. I have used Ruano de la Haza 1992 and 2000 (Bibliography, section 2) to incorporate stage directions from Z that were, for whatever reason, suppressed in M.

45. Ruano clarifies some of the play's more perplexing passages through a simple change in punctuation. One instance in which he could have applied this principle but did not involves the punctuation of verses 237–242: "Fuera, más que muerte fiera, / ira, rabia y dolor fuerte; / fuera muerte—desta suerte / su rigor he ponderado—, / pues dar vida a un desdichado / es dar a un dichoso muerte." After a personal correspondence with Ruano, I have decided to read the verses as follows: "Fuera más que muerte; fiera / ira, rabia y dolor fuerte / fuera muerte desta suerte—/ su rigor he ponderado—/ pues dar vida a un desdichado / es dar a un dichoso muerte" (see p. 95 below for the translation). I am grateful to Ruano for his helpful suggestions regarding the punctuation of these lines as well as their translation.

46. First, I read *flores* (flowers) as *fuentes* (fountains) in v. 489 (p. 99), taking the cue from v. 479 (*fuentes*) as well as from v. 507 (*cristales*) of the first edition (Ruano de la Haza 1992 [Bibliography, section 2]); the allegory breaks down otherwise. Second, a similar problem occurs with the allegory of vv. 1596–1617, where, in recapitulating the four groupings (flowers-rose, gems-diamond, stars–morning star, planets-sun [p. 120]), Calderón seems to have inserted an additional pair: *signos* ("constellations," v. 1613) and *estrella* ("star," v. 1617). I find Ruano's explanation unconvincing because it turns *estrella* into a positive term, thus undermining the force of an allegory whose purpose is to praise Rossaura at the expense of Stella (Estrella). I have resolved the problem by eliminating the surplus terms. Third, because of a glitch in the transition from the first to the second edition of the play (Ruano de la Haza 1992, pp. 39–40 [Bibliography, section 2]), there is no way for Sigismund to know Rossaura's name when he pronounces it for the first time in act 3, scene 1 ("Rossaura is in my power . . ." p. 146). I correct the problem by making Bugle's comment "By God, it's Rossaura!" (uttered in Sigismund's presence, p. 143) a public one rather than an aside; additionally, and again following the first edition of the play (v. 2807), in Rossaura's narration to the prince of her life story, I insert her name into her mother's comment "Make your way to Poland, Rossaura" (p. 145). Fourth, I read *estorbe* in v. 2864 as *estorbé* ("thwarted," p. 145); otherwise the unaccented, subjunctive form makes the thwarting appear to come at the behest of Clothold, which clearly cannot be the case given the latter's loyalty to the king, as vv. 2870–75 confirm: "that Clothold, convinced of the importance that Aistulf marry the lovely Stella and rule jointly with her, advised me to forget my dishonor and end my crusade" (p. 145). Finally, I again follow the first edition in assigning to the rebel soldier the lines that the second edition ascribes to Sigismund: "Among the crags and thickets of the mountain hides the king" (p. 149); the change makes the rebel soldier's loyalty to Sigismund clear and prepares the way for his request for a reward at the end of the play.

47. Birch and Trend 1925, pp. 11–13; Stirling 1942, pp. 47–55; Colford 1958, pp. 16–20; Raine and Nadal 1968, pp. 16–20; Campbell 1985, pp. 232–235; Honig

1993, pp. 304–306; Clifford 1998, pp. 18–20; FitzGerald 2000, pp. 390–392 (Bibliography, sections 1a, 1b). Editors of the Spanish text either ignore the coincidence, as does Morón Arroyo 2000, p. 105n, or take care to point out that the two names refer to different people, as does Ruano de la Haza 2000, p. 126n (Bibliography, section 2).

48. Bassnett 1991, p. 121 (Bibliography, section 4).

Suggestions for Directors*

LIKE MANY CLASSICAL PLAYS, *Life's a Dream* can be productively staged with true minimalist principles. Only three settings are implied throughout the play: Sigismund's tower and surroundings (1.1, 2.2, 3.1), the royal palace (1.2, 2.1, 3.2), and a wilderness area somewhere between the two (3.3). As Ruano de la Haza has pointed out, no mention is made in either the dialogue or the stage directions of stage decor in the palace scenes, which, consequently, were prob ably meant to be played on a bare stage in front of a neutral curtain.[1] The tower and wilderness scenes imply some background elements—mountains, shrubs, and the like—but Ruano's observations are again instructive: "The function of these sets was iconic rather than realistic in the sense that they served to establish a conventional, analogical relationship with the place they were meant to represent."[2] A ramp leading from one of the balconies (with its detachable railing removed to permit access), perhaps decorated with rocks and branches or boulders cut from cardboard, would have been sufficient to indicate the nature of the setting to the audience. Rossaura and Bugle's descent from the mountain would have coincided with their initial dialogue, so that by the time they reached stage level they would be in a position to see Sigismund's tower.

The tower is undoubtedly the most important element of the outdoor scenes. In Calderón's day it would have been represented in the discovery

---

* Before reading this section, the reader may wish to review the description of Comedia staging techniques offered in section 2 of the Introduction, pp. 18–19.

space, or "inner stage," on the first level of the *vestuario,* although in 3.1 there is a spatial inversion through which the interior of the tower comes to be represented on the main stage while the soldiers who break down the door enter from the discovery space.[3] In the first scene the dialogue and the sound of chains would have been all that was necessary to transform the discovery space into a tower; the dim lantern that serves Sigismund—visible against the darker ambient light of the inner stage—and the animal skins in which he is dressed would have indicated the poverty of his surroundings. In 3.1 Bugle immediately mentions that he is in prison, thus clarifying the spatial inversion that has taken place.

By the seventeenth century, sparseness of stage decor had come to stand in inverse relation to richness and diversity of costume. It has even been suggested that the lavish costumes represented a certain draw to spectators, who were bound by strict sumptuary laws that did not apply to actors on the stage.[4] In any case, it would appear that Calderón intends the wardrobe of *Life's a Dream* to be taken seriously because he devotes a large portion of the minimal stage directions to its description. In addition to indicating setting (at least as much as stage scenery does), the play's wardrobe also identifies certain symbolic aspects of the characters. Rossaura appears in three different outfits (a male traveler in 1.1, a lady-in-waiting in 2.1, and a half-man, half-woman soldier in 3.3) and Sigismund in two (animal skins in 1.1, 2.2, 3.1, 3.3, and a prince in 2.1), indicating the inner conflicts that bring them together and link them to the image of the hippogriff. Vasily appears both as the elderly king and, significantly, cloaked in disguise in 2.2, an act viewed as beneath the dignity of a monarch (hence Clothold's surprised reaction). Other important wardrobe items are the pistol carried by Clothold and the masks worn by the soldiers in 1.1, and the hat worn by the duke that so offends Sigismund in 2.1. Nothing indicates that Clothold or Aistulf would have worn anything contrary to what would be expected of a duke and a king's minister. The same goes for Stella, who would have worn the outfit of a princess; for Bugle, who would have dressed in a simple, perhaps ragged outfit reflecting his lowly social standing; and for the various guards, servants, musicians, and soldiers who appear throughout the play. Two important props are the sword with which Rossaura makes her entrance in 1.1 and the locket that Aistulf wears in 1.2 and 2.1. The sword links Rossaura to Clothold while the locket links her to the duke, and neither can be eliminated without seriously marring the visual complement they offer to the play's dialogue.

These, then, are the minimal conditions necessary for performing the play today and those in which it most likely would have been performed in Calderón's time. Contemporary directors, of course, should feel free to modify and elaborate as much as their tastes dictate and their budgets permit. If there is any indicator of a play's greatness, it is its ability to constantly refashion itself in the eyes of posterity. Elegant sets, advanced lighting techniques, and a rich musical score would all add to the performance of *Life's a Dream*. My only suggestion in this regard would be to maintain the basic visual oppositions that complement the play's verbal imagery. Calderón was a great lover of contrasts, and he builds them into the stage directions: between the neutral palace and the wild mountainside, between Rossaura's initial entry atop the mountain and her resting point at stage level, between Sigismund's dark tower and the light he carries, between the diverse costumes worn by the same character, and so on. The specific elements that form the contrasts may by freely changed to represent different or more modern settings, but the contrasts themselves can be profitably maintained in any performance. Whether Rossaura descends from a mountaintop or from the rooftop of an apartment building matters little as long as the essential vertical opposition is maintained. Likewise, if Sigismund's role as prince is to be transformed into that of a modern businessman, then an appropriate substitute for the animal skins he wears in the tower should be used to contrast with his business suit.

Happily for directors and actors, the minimal number of stage directions (even in my translation, which adds significantly to those of the original) gives ample freedom in molding not just the superficial characteristics of the performance but the way in which the play will be interpreted. The character Bugle, for example, given how little is known about him (How old is he? Why is he in the service of Rossaura at the beginning of the play? How does he intuit the relationship between Rossaura and Clothold? and so on), represents a virtual blank slate in which the actor's creative talents can truly shine.[5] The way he pronounces a certain line or combines it with a gesture can make a drastic difference in reception. Regarding such issues, it may prove useful to read the thoughtful article by Colin Thompson, which mentions a number of passages where speech modulation, intonation, and gestures are likely to have a great impact.[6] What follows is an elaboration and expansion of Thompson's list.

The deep oedipal rivalry between the king and the prince, so crucial to the play's plot and symbolism, is a gold mine for psychologically oriented actors. In the prince's first encounter with his father in 2.1, the king's language and gestures might easily be played as a provocation designed to assure the prince's failure, a failure that would both justify the king's original decision to jail Sigismund and assuage his conscience when he returns him to the tower (and thus assure that Vasily remains in power). Conversely, the actor who plays Sigismund might reflect on the fact that the prince's confrontational nature in this exchange and, in general, his barbaric conduct throughout the court scene of 2.1 may be partially a result of the drug cocktail he is made to drink at the beginning of the act.[7]

Another father-son scene ripe for interpretation comes in the much disputed moment at the end of the play in which Sigismund apparently repents: "But I—inferior to him in years, valor, and learning—shall succeed where he failed. Rise, my lord, and give me your hand; now that heaven has revealed the error in your attempts to overcome it, my neck humbly awaits your vengeance. I am at your mercy" (p. 151; see pp. 35–36 for a discussion of the scene). The precise way in which the actor interprets these lines and what he does in the all-important pauses between the sentences (Does he anguish over the decision? Does he avoid eye contact with his father? Does he give him a paternalistic pat on the shoulder? Does he kneel upon saying "I am at your mercy"? and so on) will have a major impact on the audience's interpretation of this crucial scene.

Similar pivotal scenes take place between Rossaura and Clothold in 1.1 and 3.2, where the many double entendres seem to suggest that Rossaura has intuited her relationship to Clothold and may be attempting to force a confession from him (see Introduction, p. 24); between Aistulf and Sigismund in 2.1, where the duke's loaded language seems intent on provoking the prince's ire and thus dooming his chances to become king; and in the encounter between Aistulf and Stella in 1.2, similarly charged with double entendres and sarcasm (see Introduction, p. 26).

One final note regarding reception. Depending on the venue, some of the underlined words in the text may not be familiar to all audience members, and directors may wish to substitute them with the suggestions found in brackets at the end of the Glossary entries. If the original terms are maintained, care should be taken to coach the actress who plays Rossaura so that, when she pronounces the all-important *hippogriff* in scene 1, it does not come out sounding like *hypocrite*. Suggestions for the correct pronunciation of proper names are found in brackets at the end of the entries explaining the character names (Translator's Notes, pp. 56–60).

NOTES

1. Ruano de la Haza 1987, p. 57 (Bibliography, section 8).
2. Ibid., pp. 51–52.
3. Ibid., p. 58.
4. Ruano de la Haza and Allen 1994, p. 298 (Bibliography, section 8).
5. Ruano de la Haza 2000, pp. 64–65 (Bibliography, section 2).
6. Thompson 1994 (Bibliography, section 8).
7. Ruano de la Haza 2000, pp. 39–42 (Bibliography, section 2); see also the entry under "henbane" in the Glossary.

Selected Bibliography

৵৶৵

NOTE: This Bibliography is intended both as a list of works cited and as suggestions for further reading; it thus includes items not specifically mentioned in the introductory materials.

1. PREVIOUS ENGLISH VERSIONS OF *LA VIDA ES SUEÑO*

1A. TRANSLATIONS

Appelbaum, Stanley. 2002. *Life Is a Dream*. Mineola, NY: Dover.

Birch, Frank, and J. B. Trend. 1925. *Life's a Dream*. Cambridge: W. Heffer and Sons.

Campbell, Roy. 1985 [1959]. *Life Is a Dream*. In *Life Is a Dream and Other Spanish Classics*. Ed. Eric Bentley. New York: Applause Theatre. 219–292.

Clifford, John. 1998. *Life Is a Dream*. London: Nick Hern.

Colford, William E. 1958. *Life Is a Dream*. Woodbury, NY: Barron's Educational Series.

Edwards, Gwynne. 1991. *Life Is a Dream*. In *Calderón. Plays: One*. London: Methuen. 101–200.

Honig, Edwin. 1993 [1970]. *Life Is a Dream*. In *Calderón de la Barca: Six Plays*. New York: Iasta, 1993. 287–364. [Reprinted 1985 in *Our Dramatic Heritage*. Ed. Philip G. Hill. Vol. 2, *The Golden Age*. Rutherford, NJ: Fairleigh Dickinson University Press. 453–490.]

Huberman, Edward, and Elizabeth Huberman. 1962. *Life Is a Dream*. In *Spanish Drama*. Ed. Ángel Flores. New York: Bantam. 191–242. [Reprinted 1963 in *The Golden Age*. Ed. Norris Houghton. Laurel Masterpieces of Continental Drama 1. New York: Dell. 83–147; and 1991 in *Great Spanish Plays in English Translation*. Ed. Angel Flores. New York: Dover. 191–242.]

Mac-Carthy, Denis Florence. 1873. *Life Is a Dream*. In *Calderón's Dramas*. London: Henry S. King. 1–116. [Revised and reprinted 1961 in *Calderón de la Barca: Six Plays*. Ed. Henry W. Wells. New York: Las Américas. 13–95.]

Oxenford, John. 1842. *Life Is a Dream*. In *The Monthly Magazine* 549: 255–270, 550: 389–410, 551: 470–489.

Raine, Kathleen, and R. M. Nadal. 1968. *Life's a Dream: A Play in Three Acts*. London: Hamish Hamilton.

Stirling, William F. 1942. *Life Is a Dream: A Play in Three Acts*. Ediciones "1616." Havana: La Verónica.

Trench, Richard Chenevix. 1856. *Life's a Dream*. In *Calderon: His Life and Genius With Specimens of His Plays*. New York: Redfield. 117–169. [An incomplete translation, reprinted 1970 with slight modifications (but still incomplete) in *An Essay on the Life and Genius of Calderon*. New York: Haskell House. 152–194.]

1B. LOOSE TRANSLATIONS AND ADAPTATIONS

FitzGerald, Edward. 2000 [1865]. *Such Stuff as Dreams Are Made Of*. In *Eight Dramas of Calderón*. Urbana: University of Illinois Press. 375–440.

Mandel, Oscar. 1988. *Sigismund, Prince of Poland: A Baroque Entertainment*. Lanham, MD: University Press of America.

Mitchell, Adrian, and John Barton. 1990. *Life's a Dream*. Woodstock, IL: Dramatic Publishing Company.

Williamson, Laird. 2001 [1998]. *Life Is a Dream: A New Adaptation*. Ashland, OR: Oregon Shakespeare Festival.

2. MAJOR SPANISH CRITICAL EDITIONS OF *LA VIDA ES SUEÑO*

Buchanan, Milton A. 1909. Toronto: University of Toronto Library.

Cilveti, Angel L. 1970. Salamanca: Anaya.

Hartzenbusch, Juan Eugenio. 1918 [1848]. In *Comedias de Don Pedro Calderón de la Barca*. Vol. 1. Biblioteca de Autores Españoles 7. Madrid: Rivadeneyra. 1–19.

Krenkel, Max. 1881. In *Klassische Bühnendichtungen der Spanier*. Vol. 1. Leipzig: Johann Ambrosius Barth. 37–154. (Volume includes *El príncipe constante*.)

Morón Arroyo, Ciriaco. 2000 [1976]. 27th ed. Letras Hispánicas 57. Madrid: Cátedra.

Riquer, Martín de. 1945. Barcelona: Juventud.

Rodríguez Cuadros, Evangelina. 1987. Madrid: Espasa-Calpe.

Ruano de la Haza, J. M. 1992. *La primera versión de* La vida es sueño, *de Calderón*. Hispanic Studies TRAC 5. Liverpool: Liverpool University Press.

———. 2000 [1994]. 2nd ed. Clásicos Castalia 208. Madrid: Castalia.

Rull, Enrique. 1980. Madrid: Alhambra. (Volume includes the *loa* and *auto sacramental* of the same title.)

Sloman, Albert E. 1961. Manchester: Manchester University Press.

Valverde, José María. 1981. Barcelona: Planeta. (Volume includes the *auto sacramental* of the same title.)

Vega García-Luengos, Germán, Don W. Cruickshank, and J. M. Ruano de la Haza. 2000. *La segunda versión de* La vida es sueño, *de Calderón*. Hispanic Studies TRAC 19. Liverpool: Liverpool University Press.

3. POETRY AND POETICS

Alonso, Dámaso. 1993. *Poesía española: ensayo de métodos y límites estilísticos.* 5th ed. Madrid: Gredos.

Aristotle. 1961. *Poetics.* Trans. S. H. Butcher. New York: Hill and Wang.

Baehr, Rudolf. 1970. *Manual de versificación española.* Trans. K. Wagner and F. López Estrada. Madrid: Gredos.

Greenblatt, Stephen, gen. ed. 1997. *The Norton Shakespeare, Based on the Oxford Edition.* Ed. Walter Cohen, Jean E. Howard, and Katherine Eisaman Maus. New York: W. W. Norton.

Kayser, Wolfgang. 1954. *Interpretación y análisis de la obra literaria.* Trans. María D. Mouton and V. García Yebra. Biblioteca Románica Hispánica. Madrid: Gredos.

Kinzie, Mary. 1999. *A Poet's Guide to Poetry.* Chicago: University of Chicago Press.

Mallarmé, Stéphane. 1965 [1884]. "A Léo d'Orfer." In *Correspondance.* Ed. Henri Mondor and Lloyd James Austin. Vol. 2. Paris: Gallimard. 266.

Navarro Tomás, T. 1991. *Métrica española.* Barcelona: Labor.

Rivers, Elias L. 1988. *Renaissance and Baroque Poetry of Spain With English Prose Translations.* Prospect Heights, IL: Waveland.

Vega Carpio, Lope Félix de. 1989. *Arte nuevo de hacer comedias en este tiempo, dirigido a la Academia de Madrid.* In *Antología del teatro del Siglo de Oro.* Ed. Eugenio Suárez-Galbán Guerra. Madrid: Orígenes. 779–789.

Williamsen, Vern G. 1984. "Rhyme as a Form of Audible 'Sign' in Two Calderonian Plays." *Neophilologus* 68: 546–556.

4. LINGUISTICS AND TRANSLATION THEORY

Bassnett, Susan. 1991. "Translating Dramatic Texts." In *Translation Studies.* Rev. ed. London: Routledge. 120–132.

Frota, Sónia, and Marina Vigário. 2001. "On the Correlates of Rhythmic Distinctions: The European / Brazilian Portuguese Case." *Probus* 13: 247–275.

Grabe, Esther, and Ee Ling Low. 2002. "Durational Variability in Speech and the Rhythm Class Hypothesis." In *Laboratory Phonology 7.* Ed. Carlos Gussenhoven and Natasha Warner. Berlin: Mouton de Gruyter. 515–546.

Lesser, Wendy. 2002. "The Mysteries of Translation." *Chronicle of Higher Education* 49, 5: B5.

Whitley, M. Stanley. 1986. *Spanish/English Contrasts: A Course in Spanish Linguistics.* Washington, DC: Georgetown University Press.

Cuadernos de Teatro Clásico 4 (1989) includes the following important studies:

Dixon, Victor. "Arte nuevo de traducir comedias en este tiempo: hacia una versión inglesa de *Fuenteovejuna.*" 11–25.

Edwards, Gwynne. "La traducción de textos clásicos dramáticos españoles al inglés." 27–43.

Gitlitz, David. "Confesiones de un traductor." 45–52.

MacKenzie, Ann L. "*La cisma de Inglaterra*: dos versiones inglesas del monólogo de Carlos sobre Ana Bolena." 53–77.

McGaha, Michael. "Hacia la traducción representable." 79–86.

Muir, Kenneth. "Algunos problemas en torno a la traducción del teatro del Siglo de Oro." 87–93.

Paterson, Alan K.G. "Reflexiones sobre una traducción inglesa de *El pintor de su deshonra*." 113–132.

5. DICTIONARIES, ENCYCLOPEDIAS, AND HANDBOOKS

Ara Sánchez, Jesús A. 1996. *Bibliografía crítica comentada de* La vida es sueño *(1682–1994)*. New York: Peter Lang.

The Catholic Encyclopedia. 1908–1917. Available online at http://www.newadvent.org/cathen/.

The Columbia Encyclopedia (Sixth Edition). 2002. Available online at http://www.bartleby.com/65/.

Hartnoll, Phyllis, and Peter Found, eds. 1993. *The Concise Oxford Companion to the Theatre.* Oxford: Oxford University Press.

Real Academia Española. 1726–1739. *Diccionario de Autoridades.* Available online at http://buscon.rae.es/ntlle/SrvltGUILoginNtlle.

Rose, H. J. 1991. *Handbook of Classical Mythology.* New York: Penguin.

6. CALDERÓN'S LIFE

Alonso Cortés, Narciso. 1915. "Algunos datos relativos a D. Pedro Calderón." *Revista de Filología Española* 2: 41–51.

———. 1951. "Genealogía de Calderón." *Boletín de la Real Academia Española* 31: 299–309.

Cotarelo y Mori, Emilio. 1924. *Ensayo sobre la vida y obras de D. Pedro Calderón de la Barca.* Madrid: Revista de Archivos, Bibliotecas y Museos.

Marcos Rodríguez, Florencio. 1959. "Un pleito de D. Pedro Calderón de la Barca, estudiante en Salamanca." *Revista de Archivos, Bibliotecas y Museos* 47: 717–731.

Pérez Pastor, Cristóbal. 1905. *Documentos para la biografía de D. Pedro Calderón de la Barca.* Madrid: Fortanet.

Valbuena Briones, Ángel J. 2001. "Don Pedro Calderón de la Barca: biografía, formación y cultura." In *Calderón desde el 2000: simposio internacional complutense.* N. pl.: Ollero y Ramos. 17–35.

7. SPAIN AND EARLY MODERN EUROPE: HISTORY, RELIGION, CULTURE

Bataillon, Marcel. 1966. *Erasmo y España.* Trans. Antonio Alatorre. 2nd ed. Mexico City: Fondo de Cultura Económica.

Beardsley, Theodore S., Jr. 1970. *Hispano-Classical Translations Printed Between 1482 and 1699.* Pittsburgh: Duquesne University Press.

Selected Bibliography

Biskupski, Mieczyslaw B. 2000. *The History of Poland.* Westport, CT: Greenwood.

Caro Baroja, Julio. 1965. "Honour and Shame: A Historical Account of Several Conflicts." In *Honour and Shame: The Values of Mediterranean Society.* Ed. J. G. Peristiany. London: Weindenfeld and Nicolson. 79–137.

Castro, Américo. 1916. "Algunas observaciones acerca del concepto del honor en los siglos XVI y XVII." *Revista de Filología Española* 3: 1–50, 357–385.

———. 1954. *The Structure of Spanish History.* Trans. Edmund L. King. Princeton: Princeton University Press.

———. 1972. *De la edad conflictiva: crisis de la cultua española en el siglo XVII.* 3rd ed. Madrid: Taurus.

Curtius, Ernst Robert. 1983. *European Literature and the Latin Middle Ages.* Trans. Willard R. Trask. Bollingen Ser. 36. Princeton: Princeton University Press.

Díaz-Regañón López, José María. 1955–1956. *Los trágicos griegos en España. Anales de la Universidad de Valencia* 29: 1–374.

Dios, Salustiano de. 1999. "Representación doctrinal de la propiedad en los juristas de la Corona de Castilla (1480–1640)." In *Historia de la propiedad en España, siglos XV–XX.* Ed. Salustiano de Dios et al. Madrid: J. San José. 191–242.

Domínguez Ortiz, Antonio. 1973. *El antiguo régimen: los Reyes Católicos y los Austrias.* Madrid: Alianza.

Elliott, J. H. 1963. *Imperial Spain: 1469–1716.* New York: Mentor–New American Library.

Gerber, Jane S. 1992. *The Jews of Spain: A History of the Sephardic Experience.* New York: Free Press.

Gingerich, Owen. 1993. *The Eye of Heaven: Ptolemy, Copernicus, Kepler.* New York: American Institute of Physics.

Green, Otis H. 1963–1966. *Spain and the Western Tradition: The Castilian Mind in Literature From* El Cid *to* Calderón. 4 vols. Madison: University of Wisconsin Press.

Greenblat, Stephen J. 1980. *Renaissance Self-Fashioning: From More to Shakespeare.* Chicago: University of Chicago Press.

Huizinga, Johann. 1995. *The Autumn of the Middle Ages.* Trans. Rodney J. Payton and Ulrich Mammitzsch. Chicago: University of Chicago Press.

Kamen, Henry. 1985. *Inquisition and Society in Spain in the Sixteenth and Seventeeth Centuries.* Bloomington: Indiana University Press.

———. 1991. *Spain, 1469–1714: A Society of Conflict.* 2nd ed. New York: Longman.

Kristeller, Paul Oskar. 1979. *Renaissance Thought and Its Sources.* New York: Columbia University Press.

López Piñero, José María. 1979. *Ciencia y técnica en la sociedad española de los siglos XVI y XVII.* Barcelona: Labor.

McCluskey, Stephen C. 1988. *Astronomers and Cultures in Early Medieval Europe.* Cambridge: Cambridge University Press.

Murillo, L. A. 1990. *A Critical Introduction to* Don Quixote. New York: Peter Lang.

O'Callaghan, Joseph F. 1975. *A History of Medieval Spain.* Ithaca: Cornell University Press.

Ozment, Steven E. 1980. *The Age of Reform (1250–1550): An Intellectual and Religious History of Late Medieval and Reformation Europe.* New Haven: Yale University Press.

Pennington, D. H. 1989. *Europe in the Seventeenth Century.* 2nd ed. London: Longman.

Rabil, Albert, ed. 1988. *Renaissance Humanism: Foundations, Forms, and Legacy.* Philadelphia: University of Pennsylvania Press.

Seznec, Jean. 1953. *The Survival of the Pagan Gods: The Mythological Tradition and Its Place in Renaissance Humanism and Art.* Trans. Barbara F. Sessions. Bollingen Ser. 38. Princeton: Princeton University Press.

Spitzer, Leo. 1980. "El barroco español." In *Estilo y estructura en la literatura española.* Barcelona: Crítica. 310–325.

Vernet Ginés, Juan. 1974. *Astrología y astronomía en el Renacimiento.* Barcelona: Ariel.

8. THE SPANISH COMEDIA AND *LIFE'S A DREAM*: CONTEXT, PERFORMANCE, EDITING, INTERPRETATION

Abel, Lionel. 1963. "Metatheatre: Shakespeare and Calderón." In *Metatheatre: A New View of Dramatic Form.* New York: Hill and Wang. 59–72.

Alcalá-Zamora, José. 1978. "Despotismo, libertad política y rebelión popular en el pensamiento calderoniano de *La vida es sueño.*" *Cuadernos de Investigación Histórica* 2: 39–113.

Allen, John J. 1983. *The Reconstruction of a Spanish Golden Age Playhouse: El Corral del Príncipe, 1583–1744.* Gainesville: University Presses of Florida.

———. 1993. "Staging." In *The Prince in the Tower: Perceptions of* La vida es sueño. Ed. Frederick A. De Armas. Lewisburg, PA: Bucknell University Press. 27–38.

———. 1996. "La división de la comedia en cuadros." In *En torno al teatro del Siglo de Oro: actas de las Jornadas XII–XIII celebradas en Almería.* Ed. José Berbel et al. Almería: Instituto de Estudios Almerienses. 85–94.

———. 2001. "Staging Calderón With the TESO Data Base." *Bulletin of the Comediantes* 53, 1: 15–39.

Baczynska, Beata. 1991. "La recepción de *La vida es sueño* en Polonia." *Castilla* 16: 19–38.

Balachov, Nikolai Ivanovich. 1969. "Les thèmes slaves chez Calderón et la question renaissance-baroque dans la littérature espagnole." In *Actes du Ve congrès de l'Association international de littérature comparée, Belgrade 1967.* Ed. Nikola Banasevic. Amsterdam: Swets and Zeitlinger. 119–124.

Bandera, Cesáreo. 1967. "El itinerario de Segismundo en *La vida es sueño.*" *Hispanic Review* 35: 69–84.

———. 1971. "Significación de Clarín en *La vida es sueño.*" *Atlántida* 9: 638–646.

Blanco Asenjo, R. 1870. "Hamlet y Segismundo." *Boletín—Revista de la Universidad de Madrid* 3: 219–230.

Bradburn-Ruster, Michael. 1997. "Awakening From the Dream: Calderón and the Perennial Philosophy." *Bulletin of the Comediantes* 49, 1: 35–54.

Brody, Ervin C. 1969. "Poland in Calderón's *Life Is a Dream*: Poetic Illusion or Historical Reality?" *Polish Review* 14, 2: 21–62.

Bueno, Lourdes. 1999. "Rosaura o la búsqueda de la propia identidad en *La vida es sueño.*" *Bulletin of Hispanic Studies* (Glasgow) 76: 365–382.

Callois, Roger. 1966. "Logical and Philosophical Problems of the Dream." In *The Dream and Human Societies.* Ed. G. E. von Grunebaum and Roger Callois. Berkeley: University of California Press. 23–52.

Carrera Artau, Tomás. 1927. "La filosofía de la libertad en *La vida es sueño,* de Calderón." In *Estudios eruditos in memoriam de Adolfo Bonilla y San Martín.* Vol. 1. Ed. Lucio Gil Fagoaga and Gerhard Moldenhauer. Madrid: Facultad de Filosofía y Letras de la Universidad Central. 151–179.

Cascardi, Anthony J. 1984. "*La vida es sueño*: Calderón's Idea of a Theatre." In *The Limits of Illusion: A Critical Study of Calderón.* Cambridge: Cambridge University Press. 11–23.

Cilveti, Angel L. 1973. "La función de la metáfora en *La vida es sueño.*" *Nueva Revista de Filología Hispánica* 22: 17–38.

Connolly, Eileen M. 1972. "Further Testimony in the Rebel Soldier Case." *Bulletin of the Comediantes* 24: 11–15.

Correa, Gustavo. 1958. "El doble aspecto de la honra en el teatro del siglo XVII." *Hispanic Review* 26: 99–107.

Cotarelo y Mori, Emilio. 1914. "Don Diego Jiménez de Enciso y su teatro." *Boletín de la Real Academia Española* 1: 209–248, 385–415, 510–550.

Cruickshank, Don William, and J. E. Varey. 1973. *Comedias: A Facsimile Edition With Textual and Critical Studies.* 19 vols. Farnborough, Eng.: Gregg International.

De Armas, Frederick A. 1986. *The Return of Astraea: An Astral-Imperial Myth in Calderón.* Lexington: University Press of Kentucky.

———. 1987. "Icons of Saturn: Astrologer-Kings in Calderón's *comedias.*" *Forum for Modern Language Studies* 23: 117–130.

———. 1990. "The Hyppogryph as Vehicle: Layers of Myth in *La vida es sueño.*" In *Estudios en Homenaje a Enrique Ruiz-Fornells.* Ed. Juan Fernández Jiménez et al. Erie, PA: ALDEEU. 18–26.

———, ed. 1993. *The Prince in the Tower: Perceptions of* La vida es sueño. Lewisburg, PA: Bucknell University Press.

———. 2001. "Segismundo/Philip IV: The Politics of Astrology in *La vida es sueño.*" *Bulletin of the Comediantes* 53, 1: 83–100.

Durán, Manuel, and Roberto González Echevarría, eds. 1976. *Calderón y la crítica: historia y antología.* 2 vols. Madrid: Gredos.

Egginton, William. 2000. "Psychoanalysis and the Comedia: Skepticism and the Paternal Function in *La vida es sueño.*" *Bulletin of the Comediantes* 52, 1: 97–122.

Farinelli, Arturo. 1916. *La vita è un sogno.* 2 vols. Turin: Fratelli Bocca.

Feal, Gisèle, and Carlos Feal-Deibe. 1974. "Calderón's *Life Is a Dream*: From Psychology to Myth." *Hartford Studies in Literature* 6: 1–28.

Febrer, Mateo. 1934. "Los problemas filosóficos en *La vida es sueño.*" *Contemporánea* 5: 86–101, 262–278.

Ferdinandy, Miguel de. 1961. "El príncipe preso: una perspectiva mítica en la historia de España." In *En torno al pensar mítico.* Berlin: Colloquium. 220–237.

Fischer, Susan L. 2001. "Del texto 'original' al espectáculo actual: la fuerza de la intertextualidad en *La vida es sueño.*" *Hispanic Review* 69: 209–237.

Flasche, Hans, ed. 1971. *Calderón de la Barca.* Darmstadt: Wissenschatliche Buchgesellschaft.

Fox, Dian. 1986. *Kings in Calderón: A Study in Characterization and Political Theory.* London: Tamesis.

———. 1989. "In Defense of Segismundo." *Bulletin of the Comediantes* 41, 1: 141–154.

Frenzel, Elisabeth. 1970. *Stoff der Weltliteratur.* Stuttgart: Alfred Kröner.

Galmés de Fuentes, Álvaro. 1986. "Una leyenda oriental y *La vida es sueño* de Calderón de la Barca." In *Studia in honorem prof. M. de Riquer.* Vol. 1. Ed. Carlos Alvar et al. Barcelona: Quaderns Crema. 299–309.

García Bacca, Juan David. 1964. "Sentido 'dramático' de la filosofía española: *La vida es sueño,* en tres jornadas filosóficas." In *Introducción literaria a la filosofía.* Caracas: Universidad Central de Venezuela. 227–268.

García Barroso, Manuel. 1974. "*La vie est un songe*: Un essai psychanalytique." *Revue Française de Psychanalyse* 38, 5–6: 1155–70.

García Lorenzo, Luciano, ed. 1983. *Calderón: Actas del Congreso Internacional sobre Calderón y el teatro español del Siglo de Oro. (Madrid, 8–13 de junio de 1981).* 3 vols. Madrid: Consejo Superior de Investigación Científica.

Gennaro, Giuseppe de, ed. 1983. *Colloquium Calderonianum Internationale. L'Aquila 16–19 settembre 1981.* L'Aquila: Università dell'Aquila, 1983.

Ginard de la Rosa, Rafael. 1881. "*La vida es sueño*: consideraciones críticas." In *Homenaje a Calderón.* Ed. Nicolás González. Madrid: Nicolás González. 287–339.

———. 1895. "*La vida es sueño,* comedia de don Pedro Calderón de la Barca. Estudio crítico." In *Hombres y obras.* Madrid: Fernando Fe. 5–150.

Halkhoree, P. 1972. "A Note on the Ending of Calderón's *La vida es sueño.*" *Bulletin of the Comediantes* 24: 8–11.

Hall, H. B. 1968. "Segismundo and the Rebel Soldier." *Bulletin of Hispanic Studies* 45: 189–200.

———. 1969. "Poetic Justice in *La vida es sueño*: A Further Comment." *Bulletin of Hispanic Studies* 46: 128–131.

Hall, J. B. 1982. "The Problem of Pride and the Interpretation of Evidence in *La vida es sueño.*" *Modern Language Review* 77: 339–347.

Hartzenbusch, Juan Eugenio. 1924. "Prólogo del colector." In *Comedias escogidas de Fray Gabriel Téllez (El maestro Tirso de Molina).* Ed. Juan Eugenio Hartzenbusch. 7th ed. Biblioteca de Autores Españoles 5. Madrid: Sucesores de Hernando. v–x.

Heiple, Daniel L. 1973. "The Tradition Behind the Punishment of the Rebel Soldier in *La vida es sueño.*" *Bulletin of Hispanic Studies* 50: 1–17.

Hesse, Everett W. 1966. "Some Observations on Imagery in *La vida es sueño.*" *Hispania* 49: 421–429.

———. 1977. "El doble criterio de valores en la comedia." In *Interpretando la comedia.* Madrid: José Porrúa Turranzas. 131–152.

———. 1982. "*La vida es sueño* and the Divided Self." In *Theology, Sex and the Comedia and Other Essays.* Madrid: José Porrúa Turanzas. 112–126.

Hilborn, Harry Warren. 1938. *A Chronology of the Plays of D. Pedro Calderón de la Barca.* Toronto: University of Toronto Press.

Homstad, Alice. 1989. "Segismundo: The Perfect Machiavellian Prince." *Bulletin of the Comediantes* 41, 1: 127–139.

Howe, Elizabeth Teresa. 1977. "Fate and Providence in Calderón de la Barca." *Bulletin of the Comediantes* 29: 103–117.

Hurtado Torres, Antonio. 1983. "La astrología en el teatro de Calderón de la Barca." In *Calderon: Actas del Congreso Internacional sobre Calderón y el teatro español del Siglo de Oro. (Madrid, 8–13 de junio de 1981).* Ed. Luciano García Lorenzo. Madrid: Consejo Superior de Investigación Científica. 2: 925–937.

Jones, C. A. 1958. "Honor in Spanish Golden-Age Drama: Its Relation to Real Life and to Morals." *Bulletin of Hispanic Studies* 35: 199–210.

Lapesa, Rafael. 1983. "Lenguaje y estilo de Calderón." In *Calderon: Actas del Congreso Internacional sobre Calderón y el teatro español del Siglo de Oro. (Madrid, 8–13 de junio de 1981).* Vol. 1. Ed. Luciano García Lorenzo. Madrid: Consejo Superior de Investigación Científica. 169–225.

Lavroff, Ellen C. 1976. "Who Is Rosaura? Another Look at *La vida es sueño.*" *Revue des Langues Vivantes* 42: 482–496.

León, Pedro R. 1983. "El caballo desbocado, símbolo de la pasión desordenada en la obra de Calderón." *Romanische Forschungen* 95: 23–35.

Levi, Ezio. 1920. *Il Principe Don Carlos nella leggenda e nella poesia.* Rome: Fratelli Treves.

Lindau, Frederic W C. 1930. "The Don Carlos Theme." *Harvard Studies and Notes in Philology and Literature* 12: 1–73.

Lorenz, Erika. 1961. "Calderón und die Astrologie." *Romanistisches Jahrbuch* 12: 265–277.

Maravall, José Antonio. 1990. *Teatro y literatura en la sociedad barroca.* 2nd ed. Barcelona: Crítica.

Maurin, Margaret S. 1967. "The Monster, the Sepulchre, and the Dark: Related Patterns of Imagery in *La vida es sueño.*" *Hispanic Review* 35: 161–178.

May, T. E. 1970. "Segismundo y el soldado rebelde." In *Hacia Calderón: Coloquio anglogermano, Exeter 1969.* Ed. Hans Flasche. Berlin: Walter de Gruyter. 71–75.

———. 1972. "Brutes and Stars in *La vida es sueño.*" In *Hispanic Studies in Honour of Joseph Manson.* Ed. Dorothy M. Atkinson and A. H. Clarke. Oxford: Dolphin. 167–184.

McGaha, Michael D., ed. 1982. *Approaches to the Theater of Calderón.* Lanham, MD: University Press of America.

McGrady, Donald. 1985. "Calderón's Rebel Soldier and Poetic Justice Reconsidered." *Bulletin of Hispanic Studies* 62: 181–184.

McKendrick, Melveena. 1989. *Theatre in Spain, 1490–1700.* Cambridge: Cambridge University Press.

Millé y Giménez, Juan. 1925. "Una nota a *La vida es sueño.*" *Revue Hispanique* 65: 144–145.

Molho, Maurice. 1993. *Mitologías: Don Juan, Segismundo.* Mexico City: Siglo XXI.

Morales San Martín, B. 1918. "El teatro griego y el teatro español: Esquilo y Calderón, Prometeo y Segismundo." *Revista Quincenal* 6: 260–275, 343–359.

Morón Arroyo, Ciriaco. 1990. "Semiótica del texto y semiótica de la representación." In *Teatro del Siglo de Oro: homenaje a Alberto Navarro González*. Ed. Víctor García de la Concha et al. Kassel: Reichenberger. 437–454.

Navarro González, Alberto. 1977. "Segismundo y Prometeo encadenados." *La Estafeta Literaria* 607: 29–30.

Olmedo, Félix G. 1928. *Las fuentes de* La vida es sueño. Madrid: Voluntad.

Parker, Alexander A. 1957. *The Spanish Drama of the Golden Age: A Method of Analysis and Interpretation.* London: Hispanic and Luso- Brazilian Councils. [Reprinted 1970 in *The Great Playwrights: Twenty-Five Plays With Commentaries by Critics and Scholars.* Ed. Eric Russell Bentley. Vol. 1. Garden City, NY: Doubleday. 679–707.]

———. 1966. "The Father-Son Conflict in the Drama of Calderón." *Forum for Modern Language Studies* 2: 99–113.

———. 1969. "Calderón's Rebel Soldier and Poetic Justice." *Bulletin of Hispanic Studies* 46: 120–127.

———. 1982. "Segismundo's Tower: A Calderonian Myth." *Bulletin of Hispanic Studies* 59: 247–256.

Praag, J. A. van. 1936. "*Eustorgio y Clorilene, historia moscovica* (1629), de Enrique Suárez de Mendoza y Figueroa." *Boletín de la Real Academia Española* 23: 282–314. [Republished 1939 in *Bulletin Hispanique* 41: 236–265.]

Rank, Otto. 1992. *The Incest Theme in Literature and Legend: Fundamentals of a Psychology of Literary Creation.* Trans. Gregory C. Richter. Baltimore: Johns Hopkins University Press.

Reichenberger, Arnold G. 1959, 1970. "The Uniqueness of the Comedia." *Hispanic Review* 27: 303–316; 38: 163–173.

Rennert, Hugo Albert. 1963. *The Spanish Stage in the Time of Lope de Vega.* New York: Dover.

Resina, Juan Ramón. 1983. "Honor y razón en *La vida es sueño.*" *Cuadernos de Investigación Filológica* 9: 129–149.

Richthofen, Erich Freiherr von. 1970. "Espíritu hispánico en una forma galorromana, I." In *Nuevos estudios épicos medievales.* Madrid: Gredos. 147–215.

Riquer, Martín de, and José M. Valverde. 1958. *Historia de la literatura universal, II: del renacimiento al romanticismo.* Barcelona: Noguer.

Rodríguez López-Vázquez, Alfredo. 1978. "La significación política del incesto en el teatro de Calderón." In *Les mentalités dans la péninsule Ibérique et en Amérique Latine aux XVIe et XVIIe siècles: histoire et problematique.* Tours: Université de Tours. 107–112.

Rozik, Eli. 1989. "The Generation of *Life Is a Dream* From *Oedipus the King.*" In *The Play Out of Context: Transferring Plays From Culture to Culture.* Ed. Hanna Scolnicov and Peter Holland. Cambridge: Cambridge University Press. 121–134.

Ruano de la Haza, J. M. 1987. "The Staging of Calderón's *La vida es sueño* and *La dama duende.*" *Bulletin of Hispanic Studies* 64: 51–63.

Selected Bibliography

Ruano de la Haza, J. M., and John J. Allen. 1994. *Los teatros comerciales del siglo XVII y la escenificación de la comedia*. Nueva Biblioteca de Erudición y Crítica 8. Madrid: Castalia.

Ruiz Ramón, Francisco. 1990. "El 'mito de Uranus' en *La vida es sueño*." In *Teatro del Siglo de Oro: homenaje a Alberto Navarro González*. Ed. Víctor García de la Concha et al. Kassel: Reichenberger. 547–562.

Rull, Enrique. 1975. "La literalidad del 'soldado rebelde' en *La vida es sueño*." *Segismundo* 21–22: 117–125.

Rupp, Stephen. 1990. "Reason of State and Repetition in *The Tempest* and *La vida es sueño*." *Comparative Literature* 42: 289–318.

———. 1996. *Allegories of Kingship: Calderón and the Anti- Machiavellian Tradition*. University Park: Penn State University Press.

Schevill, Rudolph. 1903. "The *comedias* of Diego Ximénez de Enciso." *PMLA* 18: 194–210.

Shergold, N. D. 1967. *A History of the Spanish Stage: From Medieval Times Until the End of the Seventeenth Century*. Oxford: Clarendon.

Sloman, Albert E. 1958. *The Dramatic Craftsmanship of Calderon: His Use of Earlier Plays*. Oxford: Dolphin.

Soufas, C. Christopher, Jr. 1985. "Thinking in *La vida es sueño*." *PMLA* 100: 287–298.

Soufas, Teresa Scott. 1993. "*La vida es sueño* as Forerunner of Calderón's Mythological Dramas." *Bulletin of Hispanic Studies* 70: 293–303.

Sozzi, Mario. 1959. "La Pologne et les polonais dans le théâtre espagnol du XVIIe et XVIIIe siècles." In *Comparative Literature: Proceedings of the Second Congress at the University of North Carolina, September 8–12, 1958*. Ed. Werner P. Friederich. Vol. 2. Chapel Hill: University of North Carolina Press. 635–649.

Sullivan, Henry W. 1979. " 'Tam clara et evidens': 'Clear and Distinct Ideas' in Calderón, Descartes and Francisco Suárez S.J." In *Perspectivas de la comedia*. Ed. Alva V. Ebersole. Vol. 2. Valencia: Albatros/Hispanófila. 127–136.

———. 1993. "The Oedipus Myth: Lacan and Dream Interpretation." In *The Prince in the Tower: Perceptions of* La vida es sueño. Ed. Frederick A. De Armas. Lewisburg, PA: Bucknell University Press. 111–117.

Thomas, Lucien-Paul. 1910. "La genèse de la philosophie et le symbolisme dan *La vie est un songe* de Calderón." In *Mélanges de philologie romane et d'histoire littéraire offerts à M. Maurice Wilmotte*. Vol. 2. Paris: Honoré Champion. 751–783.

Thompson, Colin. 1994. "Calderon's *La vida es sueño*: A More Theatrical Approach." In *The Discerning Eye: Studies Presented to Robert Pring-Mill on His Seventieth Birthday*. Ed. Nigil Griffin et al. Llangrannog, Wales: Dolphin. 77–94.

Valbuena Briones, Ángel. 1961. "El concepto del hado en el teatro de Calderón." *Bulletin Hispanique* 63: 48–53.

———. 1962. "El simbolismo en el teatro de Calderón: la caída del caballo." *Romanische Forschungen* 74: 60–76.

Valbuena Prat, Ángel. 1956. "El drama de la problemática de la vida." In *Historia del teatro español*. Barcelona: Noguer. 347–364.

Varey, J. E. 1982. "Cavemen in Calderón (and Some Cavewomen)." In *Approaches to the Theater of Calderón*. Ed. Michael D. McGaha. Lanham, MD: University Press of America. 231–244.

———. 1985a. "Stages and Stage Directions." In *Editing the Comedia*. Ed. Michael McGaha and Frank P. Casa. Michigan Romance Studies 5. Ann Arbor: University of Michigan. 146–161.

———. 1985b. "The Use of Costume in Some Plays of Calderón." In *Calderón and the Baroque Tradition*. Ed. Kurt Levy, Jesús Ara, and Gethin Hughes. Waterloo, Ont.: Wilfrid Laurier University Press. 109–118.

———. 1986. "Valores visuales en la comedia española en la época de Calderón." In *Edad de Oro*. Ed. Pablo Jauralde Pou. Vol. 5. Madrid: Ediciones de la Universidad Autónoma. 271–297.

———. 1988. " 'Sale en lo alto de un monte': un problema escenográfico." In *Hacia Calderón: Octavo Coloquio Anglogermano, Bochum 1987*. Ed. Hans Flasche. Stuttgart: Franz Steiner. 162–172.

Vida Nájera, Fernando. 1944. "Las fuentes de *La vida es sueño*." *Revista de la Universidad de Oviedo* 5: 93–147.

Wardropper, Bruce W. 1960. "Apenas llega cuando llega a penas." *Modern Philology* 57: 240–244.

———, ed. 1965. *Critical Essays on the Theatre of Calderón*. New York: New York University Press.

Warnke, Frank J. 1969. "The World as Theatre: Baroque Variations on a Traditional Topos." In *Festschrift für Edgar Mertner*. Ed. Bernhard Fabian and Ulrich Seurbaum. Munich: Wilhelm Fink. 185–200.

Whitby, William. 1960. "Rosaura's Role in the Structure of *La vida es sueño*." *Hispanic Review* 28: 16–27.

Wilson, Edward M., and Duncan Moir. 1971. *The Golden Age: Drama, 1492–1700*. London: Benn.

Zaidi, Ali Shehzad. 1996. "Hidden Treasure: The Marvelous Present and Magical Reality in *The Tempest* and *La vida es sueño*." *Bulletin of the Comediantes* 48, 2: 213–214, 295–313.

Ziomek, Henryk. 1975. "Historic Implications and Dramatic Influences in Calderón's *Life Is a Dream*." *Polish Review* 20, 1: 111–128.

———. 1983. "Polonia en la obra de Calderón de la Barca." In *Calderon: Actas del Congreso Internacional sobre Calderón y el teatro español del Siglo de Oro. (Madrid, 8–13 de junio de 1981)*. Vol. 2. Ed. Luciano García Lorenzo. Madrid: CSIC. 987–995.

Life's a Dream

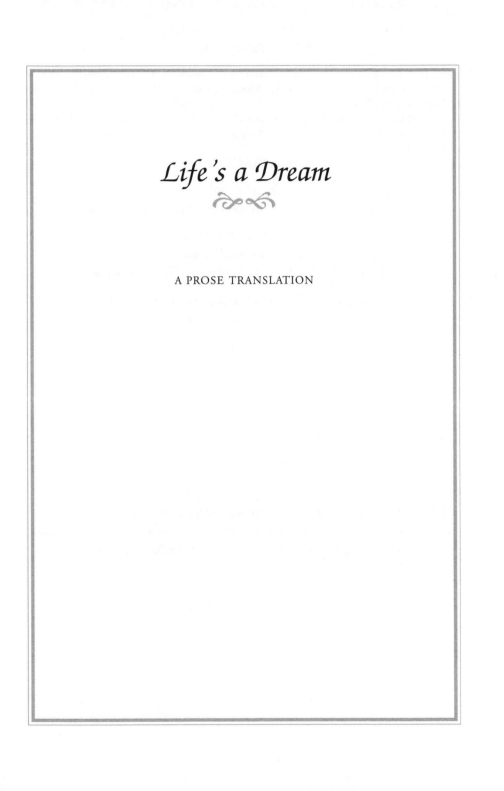

A PROSE TRANSLATION

CHARACTERS

ROSSAURA, Lady
BUGLE, Rossaura's servant

VASILY, King of Poland
SIGISMUND, Vasily's son
CLOTHOLD, elderly adviser to Vasily and Sigismund's jailer

AISTULF, Duke of Muscovy and cousin to Sigismund
STELLA, Princess of Poland and cousin to Sigismund

GUARDS
SERVANTS and COURT ATTENDANTS
MUSICIANS
SOLDIERS

SETTING

Renaissance Poland

⁓⳾

Note: Underlined words are explained in the Glossary (pp. 155–159) and character names in the Translator's Notes (pp. 56–60). The verse numbers following the scene headings refer to the Spanish original.

Act 1

SCENE 1 (vv. 1–474). DESERTED MOUNTAINSIDE AT TWILIGHT, NEAR THE ENTRANCE TO SIGISMUND'S TOWER.

Enter ROSSAURA *at the top of the mountain, disguised as a man dressed for the road. As she makes her way down the mountain, she addresses the horse from which she has just been thrown.*

ROSSAURA. Monstrous <u>hippogriff</u>, peer of the wind, you're as ill conceived as a bolt of lightning without flame, a bird without color, a fish without scales, or a beast without instinct! Where do you speed off to bucking, lurching, and bolting before the obscure labyrinth of those barren crags? Stay, then, on this mountainside and let the beasts have their <u>Phaëthon</u>; while I, a woman with no direction but that offered by the laws of destiny, shall descend in blindness and desperation the twisted face of this lofty cliff, whose scowling brow withers in the sun. Poorly, Poland, do you greet the foreigner, for you write his entrance to your sands in blood, and hardly is he come when he comes into hardship. My luck says it all, for where can an unlucky wretch turn for mercy?

Enter BUGLE.

BUGLE. Make that two unlucky wretches, and don't pretend I'm asleep back at camp when you start lamenting. For if it was two of us who left our father-land to seek adventures, and two of us who, amid misfortune and madness,

91

arrived at this spot, and two of us who were thrown down the mountain, can't I rightly complain if you make me party to the sorrow and leave me out of the tally?

ROSSAURA. I didn't want to involve you in my laments, Bugle, and take away your right to consolation through the expression of your own distress, for there is such delight to be gained from lamenting, a philosopher once said, that one should go in search of misfortunes just to be able to lament them.

BUGLE. That philosopher was a filthy drunk who deserves a thousand slaps in the face! I'd like to see how he enjoys lamenting then. But really, my lady, what are we to do now—on foot, alone, and lost at such an hour on a deserted mountainside with the sun fast headed for the horizon?

ROSSAURA. Who ever heard of such a strange turn of events? Yet unless my vision suffers from the deceptions of fantasy, I think I see some kind of building in the flickering twilight.

BUGLE. Either my desire is deceiving me, or I see the same thing.

ROSSAURA. Lying crudely among the barren crags, it's a palace so insignificant that even the sunlight barely reaches it. Its crude architecture is such that it could pass for a boulder that rolled off the mountaintop and settled at the foot of all these rocks and crags that strive toward the sun's warmth.

BUGLE. Let's draw closer and not lose more time in speculation, my lady, when it's better to be welcomed by the people who live inside.

They approach the tower.

ROSSAURA. The door—or better yet, the gloomy mouth—is open, and from its depths night, conceived inside, issues forth.

They hear the sound of chains from inside.

BUGLE. What's that sound, heavens!

ROSSAURA. I'm paralyzed, a mass of fire and ice.

BUGLE. I hear the sound of a chain; I'll be damned if it's not the ghost of a galley slave! My fear says it all.

SIGISMUND'*s voice is heard from inside the tower.*

SIGISMUND. Oh, what a miserable, unlucky wretch am I!

ROSSAURA. What's that sad voice I hear! I'm confronted with new sufferings and torments!

BUGLE. And I with new fears.

ROSSAURA. Bugle!

BUGLE. My lady!

ROSSAURA. We must flee the rigors of this haunted tower!

BUGLE. I don't have the courage to flee even if I wanted to.

ROSSAURA. Is there not a faint light in that decrepit glow, that pale star which, in faltering swoons, quivering heat, and fleeting glimmers makes the dark room even more shadowy with its feeble light? Yes, for in its flicker I can make out, even from afar, a dark prison that serves as grave to a living corpse, and, to my even greater astonishment, clothed in the skins of a beast lies a man bound in chains and accompanied only by the light. Since we can't flee, let's listen to his misfortunes from here and see what he says.

As ROSSAURA *and* BUGLE *listen, a curtain is drawn to reveal* SIGISMUND, *dressed in animal skins and seated on the floor of the tower with a dim lantern. He bears on one leg a chain that allows him some mobility.*

SIGISMUND. Oh, what a miserable, unlucky wretch am I! Please explain to me, heavens, given the way you treat me, what crime I committed against you with my birth; although if I was born, my crime is clear, and the severity of your sentence has sufficient cause, for birth itself is man's greatest crime. But I would just like to know, to ease my distress—leaving aside, heavens, the crime of birth—what else I did to merit further punishment. Weren't others born as well? And if so, what privileges were they granted that I've never enjoyed? Birds are born, and, with the regalia that decorates them in finest beauty, hardly do they attain the stature of a feathered flower or a winged bouquet when they cut swiftly through the ethereal chambers, overcoming the bond of the tranquil nest they leave behind. So how is it that I, with more soul, have less liberty? Beasts are born, and, with their coats of dappled beauty, hardly do they reflect the constellations above (thanks to divine artistry) when they become daring and cruel, and human necessity, harnessing their cruelty, makes them monsters in their labyrinth. So how is it that I, with gentler instinct, have less liberty? Fish are born, unbreathing miscarriages of algae and slime, and hardly do these scaly ships see themselves upon the waves when they begin to twist in all directions, testing the vastness of the ocean's icy depths. So how is it that I, with greater will, have less liberty? Streams are born, snakes winding through the flowers, and hardly do these silvery serpents begin to twist and turn among the blossoms when they celebrate with music the devotion of the majestic heavens that grant them passage through the open field. So how is it that I, with more life, have less liberty? *(He rises.)* My suffering rages in me like a volcano, a Mt. Etna, and I'd gladly rip the pieces of my heart from my breast! What law, what powers of justice or reason are capable of denying men the sweet privilege, the fundamental license that God grants to crystalline waters, to fish, to beasts, and to birds?

ROSSAURA. His words have filled me with fear and pity.

SIGISMUND. Who's been listening to me? Is that you, Clothold?

BUGLE. *(Aside.)* Say yes.

ROSSAURA. It's only a poor wretch—oh, miserable me!—who in these frigid caverns has overheard your melancholy words.

SIGISMUND *grabs her, his chain permitting him to step slightly past the threshold of the tower (whose door has remained open).*

SIGISMUND. Then you shall die by my hand so you won't know that I know that you know my frailties. Simply because you've overheard me, I'm going to rip you to shreds with my mighty arms!

BUGLE. I'm deaf and haven't heard a word you've said.

ROSSAURA. If you're human by birth, my kneeling at your feet will be sufficient cause for you to spare me.

SIGISMUND. Your voice has filled me with sympathy; your appearance, with wonder; and your deference, with confusion. Who are you? For although I
know so little here of the world, for this tower is both my cradle and my
grave; and although since birth, if mine can be called birth, I know only
this crude wasteland where I live miserably, a living skeleton and a breath-
ing cadaver; and although I've never seen or spoken to anyone but the one
man who frequents this place and understands my misfortunes and from
whom I know of heaven and earth; and although here—to give you more
reason to be astonished and to call me a human monster—I am, amid
bewilderment and illusion, a man among beasts and a beast among men;
and although, amid such grim misfortunes, I have studied the art of government through the example of beasts and the counsel of birds and have
measured the orbits of the gentle heavenly bodies; you alone—you—have
stayed the agony of my anger, the bewilderment of my eyes, the amazement
of my ears. Each glimpse of you increases my amazement, and the more I
look at you the more I desire to look. My eyes must suffer from the <u>dropsy</u>,
since although drinking means death, they wish only to drink more, and
thus, seeing that sight kills me, I'm dying to see. But let me see you and die,
for now that I've succumbed I can't imagine, if seeing you brings me death,
what not seeing you would bring. It would be beyond death; it would be
savage ire, rage, and intense grief—thus do I qualify its severity—for to
give life to an unfortunate wretch is tantamount to giving death to a happy
soul.

ROSSAURA. I'm so astonished by looking at you and so amazed by listening to you
that I can't think of what to say to you or what to ask you. I shall say only
that heaven must have led me here today to console me, if he who is
unfortunate can attain consolation from seeing another even more so. They
tell the story of a wise man who one day reached a point of such poverty
and misery that his only nourishment came from eating the grasses he
picked. Can there be anyone else, he said to himself, poorer and sadder
than I? And when he turned his head he found the answer, for there was
another wise man gathering up the blades that he'd discarded. Up to this
point I've lived resentful of the way fortune has treated me, and just when I
asked myself, Can there be anyone else with more miserable luck? you

responded mercifully, for, upon applying the moral of my story, I see that my sufferings would be your joys if you were to gather them up. And if by chance my sufferings might give you some relief, listen to them carefully, and feel free to take any that are left over. My name is . . .

CLOTHOLD *(Offstage.)* Tower guards! Through sleep or cowardice you've given passage to two people who've broken through the prison perimeter.

ROSSAURA. *(Aside.)* What new confusion is this!

SIGISMUND. That's Clothold, my jailer; my misfortunes are never ending.

CLOTHOLD. *(Offstage.)* Come quickly and, with vigilance, before they can defend themselves, seize them or kill them! *(In unison with the* GUARDS.*)* Treason!

BUGLE. Tower guards! You let us in here, and since we have a choice, I think seizing us would be easier.

Enter CLOTHOLD, *armed and accompanied by* SOLDIERS, *all with their faces covered.*

CLOTHOLD. Make sure you all keep your faces covered, for it's important that no one recognize us while we're here.

BUGLE. What's this, a damn costume party?

CLOTHOLD. O you, whose ignorance of this forbidden site has led you past its enclosed perimeter against the decree of the king, who has prohibited anyone from seeing the aberration that lies among these boulders; surrender your arms and your lives, or this pistol, a metallic viper, will spit forth a piercing venom of two bullets, deafening the air with its shots.

SIGISMUND. Before, O tyrannical master, you can offend or injure them, my life will become the spoils of these miserable fetters. For despite their restraint, by God, I'll tear myself to shreds with my own hands and teeth, here among these very crags, before I allow any misfortune to befall these strangers and end up bemoaning their mistreatment.

CLOTHOLD. If you know that your misfortunes, Sigismund, are so great that even before your birth you were sentenced to death by the dictates of heaven; if you know that these chains are meant to serve as a brake and rein to your arrogant fury, what are you boasting about? Guards, hide him away in his narrow cell and shut the door.

They lock him, struggling, back in the tower, and he speaks from within.

SIGISMUND. Oh, heavens, how rightly you act in stripping me of my liberty, because otherwise I would fight you like a giant who, to tear the sun off its crystal hinges, would pile mountains of marble atop foundations of stone!

CLOTHOLD. Perhaps, precisely so you won't do so, you suffer so many hardships today.

ROSSAURA. Given that his presumption has so offended you, I would be a fool if I didn't beg you humbly for my life, which lies in your power. Let yourself be moved by my sincerity, for it would be unduly severe of you to find favor with neither presumption nor humility.

BUGLE. And if humility and presumption don't move you, even though as characters they've moved and stirred a thousand allegorical plays, then I shall, neither humbly nor presumptuously but somewhere in between, ask you for your help and shelter.

CLOTHOLD. *(To the* SOLDIERS.*)* Attention!

SOLDIERS. Sir!

CLOTHOLD. Strip them both of their arms and blindfold them, so they won't see how or from where they're leaving.

ROSSAURA. *(Touching her sword, still in its sheath.)* My sword can be surrendered to you alone because, after all, you're in charge here, and it is incapable of surrendering to those of lesser rank.

BUGLE. Mine is such that it can be given to the lowest of the low: here *(To one of the* SOLDIERS.*)*, you take it.

ROSSAURA. And if I am to die, I wish to leave you, as proof of my sincerity, an instrument whose value is determined by he who once wore it. I ask you to keep it safe because, although I don't know what secret it holds, I do know that this golden sword conceals great mysteries, for I have come to Poland to avenge a dishonor with nothing else to vouch for me. *(She unsheathes the sword and hands it to* CLOTHOLD, *who cannot contain his astonishment.)*

CLOTHOLD. *(Aside.)* Good heavens! How can this be! Now my sufferings and confusions, my anxieties and sorrows, are compounded.

(To ROSSAURA.*)* Who gave it to you?

ROSSAURA. A woman.

CLOTHOLD. What is her name?

ROSSAURA. I'm obliged not to reveal that.

CLOTHOLD. Well, how do you now infer or know that it holds some secret?

ROSSAURA. The woman who gave it to me said, "Leave for Poland and, through ingenuity, deliberation, or artifice, let the noble and powerful see you with this sword, for I know that one of them will favor and shelter you." She wouldn't mention his name for fear he might be dead.

CLOTHOLD. *(Aside.)* Heaven help me! What have I just heard! Is this an illusion or reality? This sword is the one I left with the lovely Viola, signaling that anyone who returned wearing it would find me as loving as a son and as devoted as a father. So what am I to do now—oh, miserable me!—amid such confusion, when he who wears the sword seeking favor can find only death, for he comes before me doomed by the king's edict? What terrible confusion! What sad fate! What inconstant luck! This is my son; his appearance confirms what I feel in my heart, which, longing to see him, calls to my breast, beats its wings within, and—unable to break the lock—acts as he who, confined indoors, leans out the window upon hearing a noise in the street. And thus, hearing the noise without knowing the cause, my heart rushes to look out through my eyes—the windows of my soul—through which it escapes in tears. What am I to do? Heaven help me! What am I to do? To take him to the king is to take him—oh, what sorrow!—to his death, but I can't hide him from the king without violating the laws of fealty. On the one hand I am swayed by self-interest, on the other by loyalty to the king. But how can I really have any doubt? Doesn't loyalty to the king come before one's own life and honor? So loyalty it shall be, and away with honor. Besides, I recall now that he said he's come to Poland to avenge a dishonor, and everyone knows that a dishonored man is contemptible, so he can't be my son. He's *not* my son and does *not* share my noble blood. But then again, if the affront was inescapable—for honor is so fragile that it can be shattered with a single deed or blemished with a whisper—what more could a nobleman do in his defense, what more than to go looking for his remedy at all cost? He *is* my son, he *does* share my blood, for his valor is great! And thus, in such a dilemma, my best option is to go to the king, inform him that he's my son, and acknowledge that he must die. Perhaps the very conviction of my loyalty will move His Majesty to sympathy; and if I manage to earn my son's life, then I'll help him avenge his dishonor; but if the king remains steady in his severity and sentences him to death, then he will die without knowing I'm his father.

(To ROSSAURA *and* BUGLE.*)* Come with me, foreigners. But don't fear, no, that you lack company in your misfortunes; for amid such terrible doubt I know not which is worse, to live or to die.

Scene 2 (vv. 475–905). King's palace.

Enter, on one side, AISTULF *in the company of* SOLDIERS, *and on the other,* STELLA *with her* LADIES-IN-WAITING. *Music sounds.*

AISTULF. The drums and bugles, together with the birds and fountains, do well in mixing their diverse greetings in the presence of your celestial gaze, a comet in the night sky; for, alike in their music and in the great wonder they inspire, before your heavenly image the birds act as feathered bugles and the bugles as metal birds. And thus you are greeted, my lady, as queen by the drumbeats, as <u>Aurora</u> by the birds, as <u>Pallas</u> by the bugles, and as <u>Flora</u> by the fountains; because, in mocking the day that has already been banished by the night, you are Aurora in happiness, Flora in peace, Pallas in war, and queen in my soul.

STELLA. If words are to be backed up by actions, you do not fare well in pronouncing courtly compliments that are easily contradicted by such a display of military might *(Pointing to the* SOLDIERS.*)*, which I shall defiantly resist; for the flattery I'm hearing from you, as I see it, does not agree with

the severe show of force I'm observing. And take note that it's a base action, worthy only of the deception and treachery of beasts, to flatter with
the mouth and kill with the mind.

AISTULF. You're very poorly informed, Stella, if you doubt the earnestness of my
compliments, so I beseech you: listen and I shall prove that I understand
your concerns. When Eustorge the Third, king of Poland, died, he left
Vasily as his heir, along with two daughters, from whom you and I were
born. I won't tire you with details that have no place here. Clorilyn, your
mother and my aunt, who now rests under a canopy of stars in a sweeter
realm, was the eldest, and you're her daughter; next came my mother and
your aunt, the graceful Grethissunda, may God keep her a thousand years.
She married the Duke of Muscovy and gave birth to me. Now here's the
issue, my lady: our Uncle Vasily, who's already succumbing to the inevitable
contempt of time and who's always been more inclined to academic pursuits than to women, is widowed and childless, and you and I both aspire to
his throne. You contend that you're the descendent of the eldest child; I,
that I was born a man and that, even though my mother was younger than
yours, I should receive preference. We have both informed our uncle of
our intentions; he responded that he wished to resolve our dispute, and we
settled on this place and this day. With this intention I left my estate in
Muscovy; with the same intention I have arrived here and, instead of wag-
ing war against you, find that you are doing so against me. Oh, if only
Love, a wise god, would sway the masses, so unerring in their predictions,
to predict for both of us today a resolution of this matter that would make
you queen—queen of my will, that is. Thus you would find yourself—to
your greater glory—crowned by our uncle, rewarded by your own valor,
and recognized as sovereign by my love.

STELLA. To such courtly elegance my heart responds no less in kind, for I, simply
to make this imperial monarchy yours, would be happy to claim it as mine;
although my love is not altogether satisfied by your intentions, for in all you
say I fear you are contradicted by that locket hanging about your breast.

AISTULF. I'll resolve your doubts about that . . . but not now, for all those clam-
orous instruments indicate that the king and his court are approaching.

Flourish. Enter King VASILY—*an old man—and his* ATTENDANTS.

STELLA. Wise <u>Thales</u>,

AISTULF.   Learned <u>Euclid</u>,

STELLA. who governs today

AISTULF.   who lives today

STELLA. by the constellations

AISTULF.   by the stars

STELLA. and describes

AISTULF.   and glosses and measures

STELLA. their courses;

AISTULF.   their tracks;

STELLA. allow me, with obedient arms,

AISTULF.   allow me, with tender embraces,

STELLA. to be the ivy upon your trunk

AISTULF.   to surrender myself at your feet.

VASILY. Dear niece and nephew, I greet you with open arms. And, insofar as you both come here, true to my loving ways, with your own show of affection, you may trust that I shall leave no one with cause for complaint and that you will both remain each other's equal. And now, confessing weariness from the heavy burden of my years, I solicit only your silence, for the subject matter itself will solicit your amazement. You know well—and please listen carefully, my beloved niece and nephew, illustrious court of Poland, vassals, relatives, and friends—you know well that my science has earned me the nickname of Learned in world opinion; for, in defiance of time and forgetfulness, painters worthy of <u>Timanthes</u> and sculptors worthy of <u>Lysippus</u> proclaim me the great Vasily across the globe. You know also that the sciences I most study and admire lie in subtle mathematics, in whose name I rob time and exempt fame of the jurisdiction and task of making new revelations with the passing of each day. For when in my charts I see manifest the news of coming centuries, I earn the thanks owed to time for revealing what I have told. Those snowy spheres, those glass canopies illuminated by the sun's rays and encircled by the moon's beams, those diamond orbs, those crystalline globes adorned by the stars and crisscrossed by the Zodiac have received the greatest attention of my years; they are the books in which, on diamond-studded paper bound in sapphire, with diverse characters etched in gold lines, heaven records our deeds, whether adverse or auspicious. These books I read with such swiftness that I follow in spirit their rapid movements across the sky's corridors and pathways. If only heaven had taken my life as the first casualty of its ire before my ingenuity began to gloss the margins and index the pages in which I foresaw my tragedy! For even merit has a sharp edge for the unlucky, and he who is pricked by curiosity ends up destroying himself! I can say this to you with words, but my deeds will speak more clearly, so once again I ask for your silence as you listen in amazement. By Clorilyn, my wife, I had an unlucky son, upon whose birth the heavens ran out of appalling signs even before he had passed into the beautiful light of day from the darkness of the womb—a living tomb insofar as birth and death are akin. Time and again his mother, seized by the images and hallucinations of dreams, watched as a monster in human form broke forth defiantly from her entrails and, drenched in her blood, brought her death through its own birth, an inconceivable human viper. The day of the birth arrived, and, in fulfillment of the omens—for rarely or never does perverse prophecy misspeak—the child was born under a horoscope in which the sun, reddened by its blood, was entering into a wrathful duel with the moon; and, with the earth in between, the two divine torches fought with the full force of their luminous rays—a most unconventional battle. It was the greatest, most horrendous eclipse the sun has suffered since it shed tears of blood over Christ's death; and, caught in the midst of the raging fires, the earth presumed itself in the throes of extinction. The heavens darkened, buildings trembled, the clouds rained stones, and the rivers ran with blood. Under this miserable, under this fatal planet or sign, Sigismund was born and gave an indication of his nature, for, in bringing death to his mother, he said of his own savagery, "I am man, for I'm already beginning to repay kindness with cruelty." Resorting to my studies, I saw in them and in everything else that Sigismund would be the most reckless of men, the cruelest of princes, and the most perverse of monarchs; that through him the kingdom would become polarized and divided, a school of treason and an academy of vice; that, driven by his fury and wavering between bewilderment and malice, he would trample me underfoot; and that I would find myself vanquished and prostrate before him, the gray hair of my beard serving as (*Aside*: What anxiety it causes me just to say the words!) a rug beneath his feet. Who doesn't take danger seriously, especially one that arises from the studies on which his own self-worth depends? Thus, lending credence to the fates, whose soothsaying had foretold such disaster in their fatal prophecies, I determined to lock up the beast that had just been born, hoping that a wise man might rein in the influence of the stars. It was announced that the prince was stillborn, and I, ever cautious, had a tower built among the crags and bluffs of those mountains where the light of day scarcely makes its way, so heavily do the site's crude obelisks guard its entrance. The stern penalties and laws that, by public proclamation, prohibit anyone from entering the mountain's forbidden zone were made necessary by what I have told you. There lives Sigismund, in misery, destitution, and confinement; and only Clothold has spoken to him, dealt with him, and seen him. The only witness to his miseries, Clothold has also taught him the natural sciences and instructed him in the Catholic faith. Three conclusions may be drawn from all this. First, that I hold you in such esteem, Poland, that I wish to spare you the oppression and liability of a tyrannical king, because any ruler who would put his fatherland and empire in such danger could not be considered benevolent. Second is the consideration that to deprive my heir of the right he was given by human and divine sanction is not an act of Christian charity, for no law says that I, in trying to keep another from becoming tyrannical and reckless, may become so myself; yet if my son is a tyrant, to prevent him from committing crimes I must commit them myself. Third and last, I realize how erroneous it was to place easy credence in predictions of the future, since, even if the prince's inclination places obstacles in his path, they might not overcome him; because even the most contemptuous fate, the most wayward inclination, or the most perverse planet can only influence the will, not force it. And so, after hesitating and reflecting over my options, I've come up with a solution that is sure to bewilder your senses. Tomorrow I shall place Sigismund—for this is his name—without his knowing that he's my son and your king, under my canopy and upon my throne, where, acting in my place, he will govern and lead you and where you will all docilely swear obedience to him. In this way I shall accomplish three things, with which I can now respond to the three conclusions I pointed out earlier. First, if he turns out to be prudent, rational, and benevolent in complete contradiction of fate, which predicted so many things of him, you will all enjoy the reign of your rightful prince, who until now has been a courtier to mountains and a neighbor to beasts. Second, if he turns out to be presumptuous, brazen, reckless, and cruel and plays with free rein the field of his vices, I shall have fulfilled my obligation in good faith; and then, in ousting him, I shall act as any triumphant king, returning him to his cell not out of cruelty but rather as a punishment. Third, if he turns out to be the kind of prince I've just described, out of my love for you, my subjects, I shall give you a king and queen more worthy of my crown and scepter: for my niece and nephew, uniting their two claims to the throne and reconciled to each other through the sanctity of marriage, will have the title they have earned. This I command of you as king; this I ask of you as father; this I beg of you as a wise man; this I say to you as an old man. And finally, if the Roman philosopher <u>Seneca</u>, a native of Spanish soil, declared that kings are their countries' humble servants, this I beseech of you as your servant.

AISTULF. If it's up to me to respond, since it seems I'm the one with the greatest vested interest in this matter, I'll speak for everyone in saying let Sigismund come forward, for his being your son is reason enough.

ALL. Give us our prince, for we want him as our king!

VASILY. Dear subjects, I appreciate and value your goodwill. Accompany my niece and nephew, <u>Atlas</u>-like pillars of my old age, to their quarters, and tomorrow you will behold him.

ALL. Long live the great King Vasily!

Exit all. Before VASILY *can leave,* CLOTHOLD *enters with* ROSSAURA *and* BUGLE *and detains him.*

CLOTHOLD. May I speak with you?

VASILY. Oh, Clothold! You are most welcome.

CLOTHOLD. Although I should feel welcome bowing before your presence, this time, my lord, a morose and contemptuous fate has suspended routine procedure and customary practice.

VASILY. What's the matter?

CLOTHOLD. A grave misfortune, my lord, has befallen me, when it could have been cause for the greatest joy.

VASILY. Explain.

CLOTHOLD. *(Pointing to* ROSSAURA.) This handsome young man, through either boldness or ignorance, entered the tower, my lord, where he saw the prince. And . . .

VASILY. Don't fret, Clothold. If it had happened before today, I confess I would have been disturbed. But I've just revealed the tower's secret, so it doesn't matter if he knows about it as long as I allow it. But come see me later, because I have many things to report to you and much to ask of you; for you are to be, let me advise you, the instrument of the greatest event the world has ever seen. And to these prisoners, so you won't think I'm punishing your oversight, I grant pardon. *(Exit.)*

CLOTHOLD. May you live a thousand centuries, great lord!

(Aside.) Heaven has improved my luck. I won't tell anyone now that he's my son, for I can get by without doing so.

(To ROSSAURA *and* BUGLE.) Errant strangers, you are free to go.

ROSSAURA. I shall adorn your feet a thousand times with my kisses.

BUGLE. I'll just adore them from afar, for what's a letter or two between friends?

ROSSAURA. You have given me, sire, my life; and since I live in your debt, I shall be your eternal slave.

CLOTHOLD. What I've given you isn't life, for a well-born man has no life as long as he's dishonored; and given that you've come here to avenge a dishonor, as you yourself told me, I can't give you life because you bring none with you; for a life lived in contempt is no life.

(Aside.) In this way I'll spur him on.

ROSSAURA. I confess that I remain without life despite receiving it from you; but through vengeance I shall leave my honor so unblemished that my life, in surmounting all obstacles, may be recognized as your gift.

CLOTHOLD. Take back this burnished blade you brought with you, for I know that, when dyed in the blood of your enemy, it will be sufficient to avenge your dishonor; because any blade of mine—I mean "mine" in this instant, this brief period that I've held it in my power—is capable of avenging you.

ROSSAURA. In your name I arm myself with it a second time, and upon it I swear myself to revenge, even though my enemy be more powerful.

CLOTHOLD. How much more powerful is he?

ROSSAURA. So much so that I prefer not to tell you, not because I wouldn't entrust even greater matters to your prudence but because I fear losing the favor I have found in your devotion.

CLOTHOLD. On the contrary, it would be to your further advantage to tell me, for you would thus keep me from helping your enemy.

(Aside.) Oh, if only I knew who it was!

ROSSAURA. So you won't think I underestimate your trust, know that my enemy is none other than Aistulf, Duke of Muscovy.

CLOTHOLD. *(Aside.)* Good grief, that's much worse than I'd imagined!

(To ROSSAURA.*)* Let's clarify matters. If you were born a Muscovite, your natural lord cannot have dishonored you; return to your fatherland, then, and leave behind the burning tenacity that impels you.

ROSSAURA. I'm certain that, even though he's my prince, he has dishonored me.

CLOTHOLD. Impossible, even if he had dared to slap you in the face.

(Aside.) Heaven help me!

ROSSAURA. My dishonor was worse.

CLOTHOLD. State it then, for you can't say anything worse than I can imagine.

ROSSAURA. I would do so, but such is the respect with which I look upon you, the affection with which I worship you, the esteem in which I hold you that I dare not tell you that my external trappings are but a riddle, for their owner is not who you might think. So, if I am not what I appear to be and if Aistulf has come here to marry Stella, you be the judge of whether he can dishonor me or not. I have said enough.

Exit ROSSAURA *and* BUGLE.

CLOTHOLD. Listen! Wait! Stop! What confusing labyrinth is this where reason has lost its thread? My honor is besmirched, the enemy is powerful, I'm a vassal, and the offended party is a woman—show me the way out, heavens! Although I'm not sure there is a way out of such a confusing abyss when all heaven is an omen and all earth is an aberration.

Act 2

SCENE 1 (VV. 986–2017). KING'S PALACE.

Enter VASILY *and* CLOTHOLD.

CLOTHOLD. Everything you ordered has been carried out.

VASILY. Tell me, Clothold, how it went.

CLOTHOLD. In this way, my lord. With the soothing concoction you had brewed from a mixture of medicinal herbs, whose tyrannical properties and secret powers so dissipate, rob, and disorient human reasoning that they turn one into a living corpse, and whose potency robs one in his sleep of his senses and faculties—there's no reason to doubt that this is possible, for so many times, my lord, experiment has shown us, and it's true, that medicine is full of natural secrets, and there's no animal, plant, or rock that doesn't have a determined property; and if human malice has experimented with a thousand poisons in search of their lethal qualities, is it any surprise that, with just a little less potency, a poison that kills could be made to induce sleep? Not at all, for it's been demonstrated through hypotheses and proofs—with the concoction, I was saying, of opium, poppy leaves, and <u>henbane</u>, I descended to Sigismund's narrow cell. I talked with him a bit about the lessons he's been taught by the silent nature of the mountains and sky, under whose divine instruction he learned rhetoric from the birds and the beasts. To elevate his spirit to the level of the task you have in store for him, I pointed to a majestic eagle and proposed for discussion the swiftness that allowed it, in scorning the sphere of the wind, to become a feathery flare or a runaway comet in the lofty regions of fire. I praised the headstrong flight, saying, "You are, after all, sovereign among birds, so it is natural that you should consider yourself superior to all the rest." He needed no further prompting, for whenever the topic of sovereign power is discussed, he reasons with ambition and pride because his blood, of course, incites, moves, and animates him to great things, and he said: "To think that in the restless realm of the birds there is one that can command the obedience of all! In this matter my misfortunes console me, since, if I'm subservient to another, it's only by force because I would never submit of my own free will to another man." Seeing him enraged by this idea—a constant theme of his grief—I invited him to drink from the potion, and hardly had the elixir passed from the glass to his chest when he surrendered himself to the arms of sleep and a cold sweat coursed through his veins and broke out upon his body, such that, if I hadn't known it was a simulated death, I would have doubted whether he was alive. At this moment the people to whom you have entrusted the success of this endeavor have arrived and, having placed him in a coach, are taking him to your quarters, which have been prepared with the majesty and grandeur worthy of his person. They will lay him upon your bed where, when the stupor wears off, they will attend to him as if he were you, my lord, for thus you have ordered. And if having obeyed you has earned me any favor, I ask only—and forgive me my impropriety—that you tell me what your intention is in bringing Sigismund to the palace in this way.

VASILY. Clothold, your doubt is well founded, and I would like to satisfy it for you alone. The influence of my son Sigismund's star, as you know, threatens a thousand misfortunes and tragedies. I wish to study whether heaven—which is incapable of lying, especially when it's already given us, in the prince's cruel character, so many examples of its accuracy—at least softens or tempers its judgment and, won over through valor and prudence, retracts its prediction; for man ultimately has mastery over the stars. I wish to study this matter by bringing the prince to a place where he'll discover he's my son and have his talent put to the test. If he shows virtue and overcomes his inclinations, he will become king; but if his cruel and tyrannical nature wins out, I shall return him to his chain. Now you'll ask why, for the purposes of the experiment, it was necessary to bring him asleep in this way. And I wish to satisfy all your doubts. If he were to discover today that he's my son and find himself tomorrow reduced a second time to his prison and misery, given his character he would no doubt lose all hope because, with the knowledge of who he is, what possible consolation could he harbor? And thus I have tried to hedge my bets by leaving myself the option of telling him that everything he saw was a dream. In this way two things may be studied. First, his character, for he acts in his waking hours on whatever his imagination and thoughts suggest. Second, a way to console him even if he finds himself obeyed now and later reawakens in his chains, for he will conclude that he dreamed everything—and he will be correct because in this world, Clothold, everyone who lives dreams.

CLOTHOLD. I wouldn't be lacking in reasons to prove that this is not a good idea. But it's too late now, for, from the look of things, the prince has awoken and is drawing near.

VASILY. I'm going to step out. You're his mentor; go to him and, with the truth, free him from whatever confusions are besieging his thoughts.

CLOTHOLD. So you give me permission to tell him everything?

VASILY. Yes, for it may be that when he finds out, the danger will be more easily overcome because it has been understood.

Exit VASILY; *enter* BUGLE.

BUGLE. *(Aside.)* At the expense of a good beating from a blond, <u>halberd</u>-brandishing sentry whose beard matched the color of his livery, I've pushed my way in to see what's going on; for the best way to get a good seat without bribing the usher is to take charge yourself, since in all public spectacles a shallow pocket can be overcome with a deep wit and an insolent attitude.

CLOTHOLD. *(Aside.)* That's Bugle, servant to she who—Good heavens!—she who, trafficking in misfortune, has escorted my dishonor to Poland.
(To BUGLE.*)* Bugle, what's the news?

BUGLE. The news, my lord, is that the great generosity you show in your willingness to help Rossaura avenge her dishonor has encouraged her to resume dressing in women's clothes.

CLOTHOLD. A good decision, so that she not be judged indecent.

BUGLE. The news is that, changing her name and calling herself—wisely—your niece, she has enhanced her stature to such a degree that the extraordinary Princess Stella has welcomed her into the palace as her lady-in-waiting.

CLOTHOLD. It is fitting that my name accredit her honor once and for all.

BUGLE. The news is that she is hoping for the time and opportunity in which you can act on behalf of her honor.

CLOTHOLD. That's a safe bet, for time eventually settles all scores.

BUGLE. The news is that she is being pampered and attended to like a queen, thanks to calling herself your niece. And the news is that, living at her side, I'm dying of hunger; and nary a soul thinks of me, forgetting that I'm Bugle and that, when a bugle like me sounds off, it can inform the king, Aistulf, and Stella of everything that's happening, for bugles and servants are two things that don't go very well with secrecy. And if silence ever abandons me, I may become the subject of that familiar tune, *A bugle that heralds the sun / Sounds second to none.*

CLOTHOLD. Your complaint is well founded, and I shall attend to it; in the meantime, you may serve me.

BUGLE. Here comes Sigismund.

Enter MUSICIANS, *singing, and* SERVANTS, *who are busy dressing* SIGISMUND *in royal garments. The prince enters astonished by his surroundings.*

SIGISMUND. Heaven help me, what am I seeing! Heaven help me, what am I watching! The sight provokes more doubt than shock! I, in a sumptuous palace? I, dressed in fine fabrics and brocades? I, surrounded by such distinguished and gallant servants? I, waking from sleep in such an exquisite bed? I, amid so many people intent on dressing me? To say I'm dreaming is an error; I know quite well that I'm awake. Am I not Sigismund?

Heavens, reveal the truth for me! Tell me, what could have happened to my mind as I slept that I should find myself here? But whatever it was, why waste time wondering about it? Better to enjoy being served and let come what may.

SERVANT 2. He's so melancholy!

SERVANT 1. Who wouldn't be after what he's been through?

BUGLE. Me.

SERVANT 2. Go speak to him now.

SERVANT 1. *(To* SIGISMUND.*)* Shall I have them sing again?

SIGISMUND. No, I don't want any more singing.

SERVANT 2. You seem so bewildered, I thought you might enjoy some entertainment.

SIGISMUND. My sorrows can't be comforted by their voices; military marches are the only music I enjoy listening to.

CLOTHOLD. Your Highness, my lord, allow me to kiss your hand; for my loyalty will be the first to offer you obedience.

SIGISMUND. *(Aside.)* This is Clothold, so how is it that he who mistreats me in prison now treats me with such respect? What's happening to me?

CLOTHOLD. In the immense confusion of your new surroundings, your thought and reason must be plagued by thousands of doubts. But I want to free you from all of them if possible . . . *(Solemnly.)* . . . because you need to know, my lord, that you are the crown prince of Poland. If you have lived secluded and hidden from sight, it was due to the inclemency of fate, which sanctions a thousand tragedies for this realm once the kingly laurel leaf adorns your august brow. Yet trusting that, with prudence, you can overcome the stars—because a virtuous man can do so—they've brought you to the palace from the tower in which you lived while your spirit was in the power of sleep. Your father, the king my lord, will come to see you shortly, and from him, Sigismund, you'll learn the rest.

SIGISMUND. You vile, contemptible traitor! What more need I learn, now that I know my true identity, in order to exercise my pride and power from this day forward? How could you commit such treason against your fatherland by hiding me away, for you have denied me my birthright against all reason and law!

CLOTHOLD. Oh, miserable me!

SIGISMUND. You have been a traitor to the law, a sycophant to the king, and a savage to me; and thus the king, the law, and I, amid such barbaric misfortune, condemn you to die by my hands.

SERVANT 2. My lord!

SIGISMUND. Let no one try to stop me, for it would be a useless endeavor, and, by God, if you get in my way, I'll throw you out that window.

SERVANT 1. Flee, Clothold!

CLOTHOLD. *(Aside.)* Poor Sigismund, what presumption you demonstrate, unaware that you're only dreaming! *(He flees.)*

SERVANT 2. Beware that . . .

SIGISMUND. Stay out of my way.

SERVANT 2. . . . he was obeying his king.

SIGISMUND. When the law isn't just, the king needn't be obeyed; and what's more, I was his prince.

SERVANT 2. It wasn't for him to decide whether it was just or not.

SIGISMUND. You're asking for it, talking back to me that way.

BUGLE. The prince is right, and you've acted very wrongly.

SERVANT 1. Who gave you permission to speak?

BUGLE. I took it upon myself.

SIGISMUND. And who are you, pray tell?

BUGLE. A busybody, a job in which I reign supreme because I'm the nosiest person on the face of the earth.

SIGISMUND. You're the only one in this princely world I find entertaining.

BUGLE. My lord, I'm a great entertainer of all worldly princes.

Enter AISTULF, *hat in hand.*

AISTULF. Infinitely fortunate is this day, O prince, in which you proclaim yourself Poland's sun and fill its horizons with the resplendence and cheer of your divine aura, for you appear like the sun from underneath the mountains! Rise, then, and may the resplendent laurel leaf, so slow in crowning your brow, be as slow in withering. *(He dons his hat.)*

SIGISMUND. God keep you.

AISTULF. I shall forgive your meager greeting only because you don't know who I am. I am Aistulf, Duke of Muscovy, and your cousin; we must treat each other as equals.

SIGISMUND. I said "God keep you." What more do you wish? But since you don't find my greeting suitable to your high birth, next time I'll say "God damn you!"

SERVANT 2. *(To* AISTULF.*)* Consider, Your Highness, that he was raised in the mountains and treats everyone accordingly.

(To SIGISMUND.*)* Aistulf, my lord, prefers to be addressed as . . .

SIGISMUND. It irritated me the way he spoke so sternly, and the first thing he did was don his hat.

SERVANT 2. He's titled.

SIGISMUND. I'm more entitled!

SERVANT 2. All the same, it's fitting that more respect be observed between the two of you than between others.

SIGISMUND. What's it to you, anyway?

Enter STELLA.

STELLA. Your Highness, my lord, I welcome you warmly to the royal family, which gratefully receives you and desires your presence and which, despite past deceptions, wishes you an august and exalted reign and a life measured in centuries rather than years.

SIGISMUND. Tell me now, who is this imperial beauty? Who is this human goddess at whose divine feet heaven surrenders its aura? Who is this beautiful woman?

BUGLE. She is, my lord, your cousin Stella.

SIGISMUND. Stella . . . Stellar? More like Solar! *(To* STELLA.*)* Although it were well to wish me well on the wealth that I inherit, I deserve more well-wishing just for having seen you today; and thus, I appreciate your well-wishing for finding myself before such unmerited wealth. Stella—whose waking is enough to cheer the brightest shining star—what is left for the sun to do if you rise with the day? Allow me to kiss your hand, from whose snowy chalice the gentle breeze drinks in radiance. *(He moves to kiss her hand.)*

STELLA. *(Recoiling.)* Be a little more gentlemanly in the presence of the court.

AISTULF. *(Aside.)* If he takes her hand, I'm finished!

SERVANT 2. *(Aside.)* I can sense Aistulf's dismay; I must put a stop to this. *(To* SIGISMUND.*)* Beware, my lord, that it's not right to be so forward, especially when Aistulf . . .

SIGISMUND. Didn't I tell you to stay out of my way?

SERVANT 2. I'm only saying what's right.

SIGISMUND. Everything you say annoys me. Nothing is right when it contradicts my delight.

SERVANT 2. But my lord, I remember hearing you say that it's well to obey and serve what's right.

SIGISMUND. You also heard me say that I'd throw anyone who got in my way off that balcony.

SERVANT 2. Men of my standing can't be treated that way.

SIGISMUND. Oh no? So help me God, I'll prove it!

He grabs SERVANT 2 *and rushes offstage, followed by the others. A scream is heard, and all but the servant return.*

AISTULF. I can't believe what I've just seen!

STELLA. Help, everyone! *(Exit.)*

SIGISMUND. Did you see how he dropped from the balcony to the sea below? By God, I did it!

AISTULF. You should keep your rash impulses in greater check, for the difference between men and beasts is the same as that between a mountainside and a palace.

SIGISMUND. If you persist in scolding me with that smug attitude of yours, next time you might not have a head to wear your hat on.

Exit AISTULF; *enter* VASILY.

VASILY. What's going on here?

SIGISMUND. Nothing. I threw a man who irritated me off the balcony.

BUGLE. *(To* SIGISMUND.*)* Be aware that you're speaking to the king.

VASILY. The first day of your arrival has already cost a life?

SIGISMUND. He told me it couldn't be done, and I won the bet.

VASILY. It's very distressing that, when I come to see you as prince, expecting to find you mindful, triumphing over the fates and the stars, I find you acting with such severity and learn that your first deed in power is a grim murder. How can I now offer you love with open arms if I know your presumptuous embrace is trained in delivering death? Who ever looked without fear upon a naked dagger fresh from the kill? Who ever looked without emotion upon the bloody scene in which a man was murdered? Even the strongest among us responds to his instinct. And thus, recognizing your arms as the instrument of this murder and observing the bloody scene, I withdraw from your arms; and, although I had planned to encircle your neck with loving embraces, I must turn away without doing so, for I fear the grip of your arms. *(He turns his back on* SIGISMUND.*)*

SIGISMUND. I can survive without your embraces as I have until now, for when a father is capable of using such severity against me that he ungratefully casts me off, raises me like a beast, treats me like a monster, and solicits my death, it matters little that he withhold his embraces, for he has already denied me my humanity.

VASILY. *(Angrily turning back to face* SIGISMUND.*)* By God and heaven above, I wish I had never brought you into existence so as not to hear your voice and see your impudence now!

SIGISMUND. If you'd never brought me into existence, I'd have no complaint with you; but since you did, I do because you then took it from me; and although to give is the noblest and most exceptional of actions, to give only to take away later is the most despicable.

VASILY. What thanks I get for turning you from a poor and humble prisoner into the prince of Poland!

SIGISMUND. Well, what's there to thank you for in that? You've done nothing but usurp my free will. Old and decrepit, you're already at death's door, so what can you give me? Anything more than what's mine? You're my father and my king; hence all this grandeur is mine by the rights of natural law. Thus, even though you may have brought me here, I owe you nothing and could even denounce you for the time you've kept me without liberty, life, and honor; so it is you who should be thankful to me for not making you pay for what you've taken from me.

VASILY. You are barbaric and reckless; heaven has kept its word. And thus I appeal to heaven against your presumption and gall. And although you may now know who you are and understand the deception in which you have lived, and although you find yourself in a place where you consider yourself superior to everyone else, take my advice seriously: act with humility and gentleness because you might be dreaming even though you think yourself awake. *(Exit.)*

SIGISMUND. Might be dreaming even though I think myself awake? Impossible, for I feel and perceive the continuity between my past and present. And although you *(Gesturing toward the absent* VASILY.*)* may regret your decision to free me, there's no going back now; I know who I am, and you cannot—like it or not—take away my birthright to this throne. You may be used to the idea of seeing me in chains, but that was only when I didn't know who I was. But I know who I am now, and I know that I'm a composite of man and beast.

Enter ROSSAURA, *dressed as a lady-in-waiting.*

ROSSAURA. *(Aside.)* Now that I'm in the service of Stella, I'm in constant fear of running into Aistulf, for Clothold doesn't want him to know who I am or to see me because he says it's important for my honor. And I trust Clothold's intentions because I owe him a debt of gratitude for the shelter he has given my honor and life here in the palace.

BUGLE. What has pleased you most of everything you've seen and beheld today?

SIGISMUND. Nothing has completely bewildered me, for I've always known that anything is possible. Yet if I had to name something truly amazing in the world, it would be *(Gazing at* ROSSAURA.*)* the beauty of woman. I used to read in the books I had that what cost God the greatest deliberation was man, inasmuch as he is a world unto himself. Be that as it may, woman causes me more unease, for she is a heaven unto herself and is as superior to man in beauty as heaven is to earth, especially the one I'm looking at now.

ROSSAURA. *(Aside.)* The prince is here; I must withdraw.

SIGISMUND. Hey, woman, stop! Don't couple sunset and sunrise with your speedy retreat; for in coupling sunrise and sunset, warmth and cold shadow you will no doubt syncopate the day.

(Aside.) But what's this I'm seeing!

ROSSAURA. *(Aside.)* What I'm seeing inspires both doubt and belief!

SIGISMUND. *(Aside.)* I've seen this beauty before!

ROSSAURA. *(Aside.)* I've seen this splendor, this grandeur reduced to the confines of a narrow prison!

SIGISMUND. *(Aside.)* Now I know I'm alive!

(To ROSSAURA.*)* Woman—for this term is the most loving sentiment a man can express—who are you? Without recognizing you I recognize my love for you, and such is the faith you inspire in me that I'm convinced I've seen you before. Who are you, beautiful woman?

ROSSAURA. *(Aside.)* I must keep my identity a secret.

(To SIGISMUND.*)* Just a lowly lady-in-waiting to Princess Stella.

SIGISMUND. You misspeak; you are the sun on whose flame that stellar beauty lives, for it takes its resplendence from your rays. I have seen how, in the fragrant realm of the flowers, the divine rose rules over all others, empress through her greater beauty. I have seen how, in the dark depths of the learned academy of precious gems, the diamond is crowned emperor because of his greater brilliance. I have seen how, in the beautiful corridors of the restless realm of the stars, the morning star, first in rank, rules as king. I have seen how, in the perfect spheres of heaven, the sun calls the planets to congress, presiding over them as the most dazzling source of daylight. So how is it that when, among flowers, gems, stars, and planets the most beautiful govern, you serve one of lesser beauty while you—ever more beautiful and lovely—are the sun, the morning star, the diamond, and the rose?

Enter CLOTHOLD, *unseen.*

CLOTHOLD. *(Aside.)* I must restrain Sigismund, for it was I, after all, who raised him. But what's going on here?

ROSSAURA. I cherish your kindness, but silence will be my most eloquent response; for when reason falters, my lord, the most articulate is the one who knows how to keep quiet. *(She turns to exit.)*

SIGISMUND. Stop; wait! How can you presume to leave my senses in the dark like that?

ROSSAURA. I request Your Highness's permission to go.

SIGISMUND. To go so suddenly is not a request; it's called taking matters into your own hands.

ROSSAURA. Well, if you don't grant me permission, I shall have no other choice.

SIGISMUND. You'll force me from politeness to rudeness because resistance acts as a cruel venom upon my patience.

ROSSAURA. Well, even if that venom—full of fury, severity, and wrath—were to overcome your patience, it wouldn't dare attack my honor, nor could it.

SIGISMUND. You'll make me lose the fear your beauty inspires in me just to see if I can, for I'm strongly inclined to overcome the impossible. Today I threw a man off that balcony who said it couldn't be done, so have no doubt that I'll throw your honor out the window just to see if I can.

CLOTHOLD. *(Aside.)* His rashness knows no bounds. What am I to do, heavens, in the face of this mad desire that puts my honor at risk a second time?

ROSSAURA. Not in vain were the warnings that this unlucky realm would suffer, at the hands of your tyranny, terrible scandals of transgression, treason, ire, and death. Yet what can be expected of a man who—human in name only— is reckless, inhuman, cruel, presumptuous, barbaric, and tyrannical; a man who, after all, was born among beasts?

SIGISMUND. Precisely so you wouldn't insult me that way, I was polite with you, thinking I could win you over with such measures; but if my efforts mean nothing to you, then, by God, I might as well live up to your insults! *(To* BUGLE.*)* You there, leave us alone, close the door, and make sure no one comes in!

Exit BUGLE.

ROSSAURA. *(Aside.)* I'm finished!
(To SIGISMUND.*)* I'm warning you!

SIGISMUND. I'm a tyrant, remember? So your attempts to restrain me are in vain.

CLOTHOLD. *(Aside.)* Oh, what an awful predicament! I must stop him even if he kills me.

(To SIGISMUND.*)* My lord, listen to reason!

SIGISMUND. This is the second time you provoke my ire, you decrepit old madman. Do you take my anger and severity so lightly? How did you get in here?

CLOTHOLD. Summoned by the cries of her voice, I'm here to tell you to act more peacefully if you desire to rule; and you needn't resort to cruelty just because you have authority over others, because this may all be a dream.

SIGISMUND. You provoke my rage by lecturing me about reality. I'll kill you and see if it's a dream or reality!

As he goes to unsheathe his sword, CLOTHOLD *detains him and kneels before him.*

CLOTHOLD. I'm hoping this gesture will save my life.

SIGISMUND. Take your brazen hand off my blade!

CLOTHOLD. Until someone arrives who can restrain your severity and quick temper, I will not let you go.

ROSSAURA. Good heavens!

SIGISMUND. Let go I say, you decrepit madman, you barbaric traitor, or else . . . *(They fight.)* . . . I'll kill you with my bare hands!

ROSSAURA. Come quickly, everyone, he's going to kill Clothold! *(Exit.)*

As AISTULF *enters* CLOTHOLD *falls at his feet, and* AISTULF *steps between the two antagonists.*

AISTULF. What's the meaning of this, kind prince? You would tarnish your gallant blade with the blood of an old man? Return your distinguished sword to its sheath.

SIGISMUND. As soon as I've drenched it in his contemptible blood.

AISTULF. His life seeks refuge at my feet, so my arrival must be for a reason.

SIGISMUND. Reason for you to die, since with your death I'll also make you pay for the anger you provoked in me earlier.

AISTULF. I fight in self-defense and thus commit no offense against the crown.

They unsheathe their swords. Enter VASILY *and* STELLA.

CLOTHOLD. *(To* AISTULF.*)* Don't hurt him, my lord!

VASILY. What's this, swords drawn in the palace?

STELLA. *(Aside.)* It's Aistulf! Oh, miserable me, this is torture!

VASILY. What's going on here?

AISTULF. Nothing, my lord, now that you're here.

They sheathe their swords.

SIGISMUND. A great deal, my lord, even though you've arrived. I tried to kill that old man.

VASILY. You show no respect for his gray hair?

CLOTHOLD. Don't fret, my lord; my gray hair is unimportant.

SIGISMUND. It is in vain to hope that I will show respect for gray hair; why, I might even see yours *(Gesturing at* VASILY.*)* at my feet one day because I still haven't had my revenge for the unjust manner in which you raised me! *(Exit.)*

VASILY. Well, before that happens, you'll return to sleep in a place where, upon awakening, you'll believe that all that has happened to you, like everything of this world, was a dream.

Exit VASILY *and* CLOTHOLD. STELLA *and* AISTULF *remain onstage.*

AISTULF. How seldom fate errs in predicting misfortune, for it is as accurate in foretelling evil as it is inaccurate in foretelling good! What an excellent astrologer it would be if it limited itself to the harshest predictions, for there's no doubt that they would always come true! This theory, Stella, is confirmed in the case of both Sigismund and myself, for in each of us there was a different prediction. In Sigismund's case it foresaw severity, presumption, misfortune, and death, and it was right in each instance because everything has come true in the end. But in my case—where, my lady, once my eyes met your celestial gaze, of which the sun is but a shadow and the sky a mere hint, it predicted good fortune, triumph, acclaim, and wealth— it was both wrong and right; for when fate hints at favors, it's only right to expect contempt.

STELLA. I'm sure your compliments are heartfelt; yet I suspect they're intended for another lady, Aistulf, perhaps the one whose portrait you wore in the locket around your neck when you first came to see me. That being the case, your amorous sentiments are best directed toward her; go to her to claim your reward, for insincere compliments and misrepresentations are no more valid in courtship than they are at court.

Enter ROSSAURA, *hidden.*

ROSSAURA. *(Aside.)* Thank God my cruel misfortunes are finally coming to an end, for whoever suffers through this is prepared for anything!

AISTULF. I'll banish the locket's portrait from my breast to make way for your beautiful image. Where Stella's light is present, shadows have no place . . .
(Aside.) . . . nor does stellar light in the presence of the sun.
(To STELLA.*)* I'll go get the locket.
(Aside.) Forgive me, lovely Rossaura, for the offense, but this is as faithful as men and women can be when they're apart. *(Exit.)*

ROSSAURA. *(Aside.)* I was so worried he'd see me that I didn't catch anything they said.

STELLA. Astraea?

ROSSAURA. My lady?

STELLA. I'm glad it's you because you're the only one I can trust with a secret.

ROSSAURA. You're too kind, my lady, to one who serves you.

STELLA. In the short time I've known you, Astraea, you've earned the keys to my volition; for this reason and because of who you are, I'm going to trust you with a secret I'm not even comfortable with myself.

ROSSAURA. You command my absolute loyalty.

STELLA. Well, to make a long story short, my first cousin Aistulf—it should be enough to say he's my *first* because some things are spoken through thought alone—is to marry me, if in fact fortune is willing to remedy so much adversity with a single act of joy. I was distressed the first day I saw him that he was wearing the portrait of another lady in a locket around his neck. I spoke to him about it politely; he's gentlemanly and well-intentioned, so he went to get the locket and is going to bring it here. But I feel too awkward accepting it from him directly. Stay here, and when he comes, tell him to hand it over to you. I'll say no more; you're discreet and beautiful and must know quite well what it means to be in love. *(Exit.)*

ROSSAURA. If only I didn't! Heaven help me! What woman is careful and prudent enough to escape such a dilemma? Can there be anyone else in the world whom the merciless heavens assail with more misfortune and besiege with more sorrow? What shall I do amid such confusion, where it seems impossible to find a solution that comforts me or a comfort that consoles me? Since the first misfortune, nothing has happened or arisen that hasn't turned into another misfortune, and they seem to succeed one another like heirs. In imitation of the phoenix, they breed one another, living on what kills them; and their urn is always alive with their ashes. Misfortunes are cowardly, a philosopher once said, because they never seem to walk alone; but I say they're courageous, since they always push forward and never look back. Whoever is escorted by misfortunes need stop at nothing, for he need never fear that they will abandon him. I can say this because so many have occurred in my life that I've never found myself without them, nor do they tire until they find me wounded by fortune and in the arms of death. Oh, miserable me! What shall I do now under such circumstances? If I reveal my identity, Clothold, to whom I owe my life for his protection and esteem, might be offended, for he has asked me to keep quiet while awaiting his remedy to my dishonor. But if I don't reveal my identity, how can I keep up the charade when Aistulf arrives? For even if I manage to disguise my voice, my speech, and my eyes, my soul will expose them all as liars. What shall I do? But why deliberate over what to do when it's evident that, no matter how I prepare, deliberate, and think, when the moment arrives my grief will make me act as it sees fit? For no one can claim absolute rule over his sufferings. And since my soul dares not determine a course of action, let my grief culminate today and let my suffering reach its extreme, as long as I'm freed of doubting and guessing once and for all. But until then, give me strength, heavens, give me strength!

Enter AISTULF *with the locket.*

AISTULF. Here, my lady, is the locket . . . but . . . my god!

ROSSAURA. Why that look of bewilderment, my lord? Why are you so amazed?

AISTULF. To hear your voice, Rossaura, and to see you here before me.

ROSSAURA. I, Rossaura? You are mistaken, my lord, if you take me for another lady; for I am Astraea, and my humble station is not worthy of the joy caused by your confused affection.

AISTULF. Enough with the deception, Rossaura, for the soul never lies; and although mine may behold you as Astraea, it loves you as Rossaura.

ROSSAURA. I don't understand, my lord, so I don't know how to respond. All I can say is that Stella (who's at least as stellar as Venus) has ordered me to wait here for you and to ask you to hand over that locket—which seems like a very reasonable request—and to take it to her myself. Stella wishes it thus, for even the slightest of actions, if they end up compromising me, are stellar in design.

AISTULF. Try as you might, Rossaura, you're a most unconvincing liar! Tell your eyes to harmonize their music to your voice; otherwise it's inevitable that such a cacophonous instrument stutter and falter in attempting to adjust and calibrate the falsehoods of speech to the truth of feelings.

ROSSAURA. I repeat that I'm here only for the locket.

AISTULF. Well, since you insist on carrying on with this deception, I shall reply in kind. You may tell the princess, Astraea, that I hold her in such esteem that, when she asks me for a portrait, I consider it in poor taste to send it to her; rather, that she may treasure and revere it, I'm sending her the original. And you may take it to her directly, for you already bear it with you if you can bear yourself.

ROSSAURA. When a determined, willful, and courageous man agrees to undertake a mission, if he returns without reaching the goal—even if he acquires something more valuable in the process—he faces ridicule and humiliation. I'm here for a portrait, and even if I take back an original of greater worth, I'll be ridiculed. Give me the locket, my lord, for I will not return without it.

AISTULF. *(Taunting.)* Well, I don't know how you expect to take it if I don't give it to you.

ROSSAURA. Like this. *(She grabs for the locket.)* Give it to me, you ingrate!

AISTULF. Forget it.

ROSSAURA. By God, it's not for another woman's hands! *(She continues struggling for the locket.)*

AISTULF. My, you're ferocious today!

ROSSAURA. And you're a two-timing scoundrel!

AISTULF. That's enough, my Rossaura.

ROSSAURA. I'm not your Rossaura, you swine!

They continue struggling. Enter STELLA.

STELLA. Astraea, Aistulf! What's the meaning of this?

AISTULF. *(Aside.)* Oh no, it's Stella!

ROSSAURA. *(Aside.)* May love grant me the ingenuity to get my locket back.
(To STELLA.*)* If you wish to know what's going on, my lady, I shall tell you.

AISTULF. *(Aside to* ROSSAURA.*)* What do you think you're doing?

ROSSAURA. You ordered me to wait here for Aistulf and to ask him for a locket on your behalf. I was left alone, and as related topics associate freely in the mind, your talk of lockets reminded me that I was carrying one of my own in my sleeve. I decided to look at it, for people always entertain themselves with nonsense when they're alone. I accidentally dropped it on the floor, and Aistulf, who'd just arrived to give you the other lady's locket, picked it up; and not only was he unwilling to hand over the one you'd asked him for, but he also decided to take mine. And since he wouldn't give it back even when I begged and beseeched him, I grew angry and impatient and tried to take it by force. That's mine in his hand now; you can easily tell from the resemblance it bears to me.

STELLA. Let go of the locket, Aistulf! *(She takes it from him.)*

AISTULF. My lady!

STELLA. *(Looking at the locket, then at* ROSSAURA.*)* A faithful copy of the original.

ROSSAURA. Then you agree it's mine?

STELLA. How could there be any doubt?

ROSSAURA. *(Triumphant.)* Now tell him to give you the other one.

STELLA. *(Dismayed.)* Take your locket and go.

ROSSAURA. *(Aside.)* At least I got my locket back. The rest is their problem. *(Exit.)*

STELLA. Now give me the locket I asked you for; for though I don't plan to look at you or speak to you ever again, I don't want it to remain in your power, no, if only because I so foolishly asked you for it.

AISTULF. *(Aside.)* How can I get out of this awful predicament?
(To STELLA.*)* Although I should like, lovely Stella, to serve and obey you, I can't give you the locket you request because . . .

STELLA. You're a swine and a boorish suitor! I don't want it from you now because I wouldn't want to be reminded, in taking it, that I ever asked you for it! *(Exit.)*

AISTULF. Hey . . . listen . . . look . . . wait! Goddamn you, Rossaura! From where, how, or why did you show up in Poland today? You're going to end up destroying yourself and me with you! *(Exit.)*

SCENE 2 (VV. 2018–2187). THE TOWER AS DESCRIBED IN ACT 1.

SIGISMUND, *bound in chains and dressed in animal skins as at the beginning of the play, is asleep on the floor. Enter* CLOTHOLD, BUGLE, *and two* SERVANTS.

CLOTHOLD. *(To the* SERVANTS.*)* Leave him here, for his presumption will end today where it began.

SERVANT 1. I've secured the chain as before.

BUGLE. Better never to wake up, Sigismund; you'll only find yourself destroyed, your luck reversed, your counterfeit pleasure reduced to a shadow of life and a glow of death.

CLOTHOLD. People who talk as much as you do should have a nice place in which to debate. *(To the* SERVANTS.*)* Seize him and lock him away in that cell.

BUGLE. Why me?

CLOTHOLD. Because a Bugle that knows so many secrets must be kept locked away where it can't sound off.

BUGLE. Have I, by chance, tried to kill my father? No. Am I the one who threw little Icarus off the balcony? Is my death or rebirth the issue here? Does my dreaming or sleeping matter? What's your purpose in locking me up?

CLOTHOLD. You're Bugle.

BUGLE. Well, I'll call myself Horn from now on, and I'll keep quiet as befits those with horns.

They lock him in the tower. Enter VASILY, *his face hidden by a hood.*

VASILY. Clothold?

CLOTHOLD. My lord! Why does Your Majesty come in disguise?

VASILY. A foolish curiosity to see what happens with Sigismund—oh, miserable me!—has lowered me to this level.

CLOTHOLD. Behold him there, reduced to the misery of his former self.

VASILY. Oh, unfortunate prince, born under such a sad sign! *(To* CLOTHOLD.*)* Go wake him now, for the lotus he drank should be wearing off.

CLOTHOLD. He is restless, my lord, and talking in his sleep.

VASILY. What could he be dreaming now? Let's listen.

SIGISMUND. *(In his sleep.)* A proper prince is he who punishes tyrants. Clothold shall die by my hands! My father shall kiss my feet!

CLOTHOLD. He threatens me with death.

VASILY. And me with severity and disrespect.

CLOTHOLD. He wishes to take my life.

VASILY. He schemes to have me bow before his feet.

SIGISMUND. *(In his sleep.)* On the broad public square that is the great stage of the world, my unequalled valor shall make its appearance! To satisfy my vengeance, all shall watch Prince Sigismund triumph over his father! *(He wakes up.)* But—oh, miserable me!—where am I?

VASILY. *(Aside to* CLOTHOLD.*)* He mustn't see me. You know what to do. I shall listen from over there. *(He steps back and remains out of* SIGISMUND*'s view.)*

SIGISMUND. *(Touching himself.)* Is this really me? Is this me, reduced to prison and chains? Is this not the tower that is my grave? Yes. God help me, what a deluge of dreams!

CLOTHOLD. *(Aside.)* It's up to me to carry off the charade.
(To SIGISMUND.*)* Are you finally waking up?

SIGISMUND. Yes, I'm finally waking up.

CLOTHOLD. Have you been sleeping all day? You haven't woken since I left to follow the flight of that majestic eagle while you stayed put?

SIGISMUND. No, nor am I awake now, for as I see it, Clothold, I'm still sleeping. I can't be very wrong because, if what seemed so palpable and true to me was only a dream, what I'm seeing now mustn't be trusted. And it's no surprise, given I can see in my sleep, that exhaustion should lead me to dream while awake.

CLOTHOLD. Tell me what you dreamed.

SIGISMUND. Even if it was a dream, I won't say what I dreamed, Clothold, but rather what I saw. I awoke to find myself—what flattering cruelty!—upon a bed that could have been, with a bit of detail and color, a mat of flowers woven by Spring. There a thousand noblemen, bowing at my feet, called me their prince and adorned me in fine clothes and precious gems. You appeared and turned the numbness of my senses into happiness by announcing the joyous news; for although I live in misery here, there I was Prince of Poland.

CLOTHOLD. You must have given me a handsome reward!

SIGISMUND. Not exactly. With a daring and mighty spirit, I twice tried to kill you for your treason.

CLOTHOLD. Such severity toward me?

SIGISMUND. I was lord over all, and I wanted revenge on everyone. My only love was for a woman, a love I still believe to be real because, while everything else has vanished, it alone has remained with me.

Exit VASILY.

CLOTHOLD. *(Aside.)* The king has left, filled with sympathy at the prince's remarks.

(To SIGISMUND.*)* Because we had spoken about that eagle beforehand, when you went to sleep you dreamed of empire. But in your dreams it would be fitting, Sigismund, to show more respect to he who raised you with such care; for even in dreams it pays to do what's right. *(Exit.)*

SIGISMUND. This is true; so we must repress this savage character, this fury, this ambition, just in case we dream again. And that will happen sooner or later, for we live in such an exceptional world that living is no more than dreaming; and experience teaches me that he who lives dreams what he is until waking. The king dreams that he's king, and he lives under this deception commanding, planning, and governing; and his acclaim, which he receives on loan, is scribbled in the wind and turned to ashes by death. What grave misfortune! To think that anyone should wish to govern knowing that he will awaken in the sleep of death! The rich man dreams of more riches, which only bring him more worries; the poor man dreams that he suffers in misery and poverty; the man who improves his lot dreams; the man who toils and petitions dreams; the man who insults and offends dreams. And in this world, in short, everyone dreams what he is although no one realizes it. I dream that I'm here, weighed down by these chains, and I've dreamt that I found myself in more flattering circumstances. What is life? A frenzy. What is life? A vain hope, a shadow, a fiction. The greatest good is fleeting, for all life is a dream and even dreams are but dreams.

Act 3

SCENE 1 (vv. 2188–2427). The tower.

Enter BUGLE *amid darkness. He addresses the audience.*

BUGLE. In a haunted tower, because of what I know, I'm being held captive. What will they do to me because of my ignorance if they ax me because of my knowledge? To think that a fellow should be sentenced to a life of starving to death! Everyone will say I'm feeling sorry for myself. Well, they're right, because this silence, in my opinion, doesn't befit one named Bugle, and I can't shut up. My only company here, if I can bring myself to say so, are spiders and mice—what lovely goldfinches! My dreams last night filled my poor head with <u>shawms</u>, trumpets, and tomfoolery; and with processions, crucifixes, and penitents marching up and down and fainting at the sight of one another's blood. Whereas I, to tell the truth, am fainting from hunger, for I find myself in a prison where the board is bare and the menu mean. If silence is considered saintly, then Saint Secret must be my day in the <u>New Calendar</u>, for I fast in his honor and never feast! But the punishment I suffer is well deserved, for, unlike most servants, I kept my mouth shut, which is the greatest sacrilege.

A sound of drums and people is heard, and a voice speaks from offstage.

SOLDIER 1. This is his tower. Break down the door! Everyone in!

133

BUGLE. By God! They must be looking for me, for they know I'm here! What can they want with me?

Enter as many SOLDIERS *as possible.*

SOLDIER 1. Inside, inside!

SOLDIER 2. *(Pointing to* BUGLE.*)* There he is.

BUGLE. No he's not.

SOLDIERS. *(In unison.)* My lord!

BUGLE. *(Aside.)* Are these guys drunk or what?

SOLDIER 2. You are our prince; we will not accept and do not want anyone but our rightful lord, not a foreign prince. Grant us all your feet, that we may bow before them.

SOLDIERS. *(In unison.)* Long live our great prince!

BUGLE. *(Aside.)* By God, it's for real! Can it be a custom of this kingdom to take a new prisoner each day, make him prince, and then return him to the tower? Apparently so, for I've seen it happen each day I've been here. I'll have to play my role.

SOLDIERS. *(In unison.)* Grant us the soles of your feet. *(They kneel to kiss his feet.)*

BUGLE. I can't because I need them for myself, and I wouldn't do you much good as a de-solate prince.

SOLDIER 2. We've all told your father that we'll accept only you as our prince, not the Muscovite.

BUGLE. You insulted my father that way? You've got a lot of nerve!

SOLDIER 1. It was the loyalty of our hearts speaking.

BUGLE. If it was out of loyalty, then I forgive you.

SOLDIER 2. Come forth and restore your rule. Long live Sigismund!

ALL SOLDIERS. *(In unison.)* Long live Sigismund!

BUGLE. *(Aside.)* They call me Sigismund? Why, it must be the name they reserve for all their bogus princes.

Enter SIGISMUND.

SIGISMUND. Who calls my name?

BUGLE. *(Aside.)* Alas, is my time as prince already up?

SOLDIER 2. Which of you is Sigismund?

SIGISMUND. I am.

SOLDIER 2. *(To* BUGLE.*)* You impudent fool! How dare you call yourself Sigismund?

BUGLE. Me, call myself Sigismund? That's not true. You're the ones who Sigismunded me, so you're the impudent fools.

SOLDIER 1. Great Prince Sigismund—the sight of whom validates the faith that led us to proclaim you our lord—your father, the great King Vasily, fearful lest the heavens bear out a fate that says he will end up at your feet, vanquished by his own son, is attempting to deny you your rightful authority and give it to Aistulf, Duke of Muscovy. For this purpose he convened his court, but the masses learned of the events and, realizing that they have a Polish-born prince, refuse to be ruled by a foreigner. And thus, nobly overlooking the inclemency of fate, they search for you where you are held prisoner so that, with the aid of their weapons, you may break out of this tower and recover your imperial crown and scepter, stripping them from a tyrant. Come forth, then, for a numerous army of outlaws and peasants hails you in the wilderness. Freedom is within your grasp; listen to its chant.

VOICES. *(Offstage, in unison.)* Long live Sigismund! Long live the prince!

SIGISMUND. *(Aside.)* What in heaven is going on! Am I again to dream of grandeur only to see it undone by time? Am I to glimpse again the shadows and outlines of majesty and splendor only to see them swept away by the wind? Must I learn the truth all over again—that human power is born humbly of risk and lives in constant jeopardy? It shall not happen; it shall not. Look at me, once again prisoner of my fortune. And since I know that this life is all a dream, be gone, shadows, you who today feign bodies and voices before my deadened senses when I know you have no body or voice. For I don't want counterfeit majesty and splendor, no! Fanciful illusions that unravel at the slightest touch of a breeze—just like the budding almond tree whose flowers, without warning and ignoring counsel, bloom early and expire at the first cold wind, withering and tarnishing the beauty, light, and color of their rosy bonnets—I see you, I recognize you, and I know you play the same game with everyone who sleeps. I won't be fooled this time, for I've learned the truth and know that life is a dream.

SOLDIER 2. *(Sensing* SIGISMUND's *doubt.)* If you think we're deceiving you, turn your gaze toward those imperious mountains, and you'll see all the people who wait there to obey your command.

SIGISMUND. I've seen this before as clearly and distinctly as I'm seeing it now, yet it was a dream.

SOLDIER 1. Great things are always announced in premonitions, which must be what you had if you dreamt this moment.

SIGISMUND. You're right; it was a premonition.

(Aside.) And just in case it was correct, given that life is so short, let's dream, my soul, let's dream again. But this time we must be vigilant and aware that we shall awaken from this delight at the best moment; and if we keep that in mind, the truth will be easier to bear, for to be prepared for harm is to avoid it. And with the knowledge that, even if the premonition was correct, all power is borrowed and must be returned to its heavenly owner, let us stop at nothing.

(To the SOLDIERS.) Vassals, I appreciate your loyalty; you can count on me, bold and adroit, to liberate you from slavery to a foreigner. Sound the call to arms, and shortly you will see my immense valor in action. I shall take arms against my father and prove the heavens true; soon he will be at my mercy.

(Aside.) Yet, given that I could wake up before then, wouldn't it be better not to make promises I can't keep?

ALL. *(Offstage, in unison.)* Long live Sigismund! Long live the prince!

Enter CLOTHOLD, *on his way to visit* SIGISMUND *in the tower.*

CLOTHOLD. What's all the commotion, heavens?

SIGISMUND. Clothold!

CLOTHOLD. My lord!

(*Aside.*) My life will be the test of his cruelty.

BUGLE. (*Aside.*) I'll bet he hurls him off the mountain. (*Exit.*)

CLOTHOLD. I come before your regal feet, certain of my death. (*He kneels before* SIGISMUND.)

SIGISMUND. On your feet, father, on your feet; you will be the compass and guide to whom I entrust my achievements, for I know that I owe my upbringing to your ceaseless loyalty. Let me embrace you.

CLOTHOLD. (*He remains on his knees.*) What are you saying?

SIGISMUND. That I'm dreaming, and that I want to do what's right, for it pays to do what's right even in dreams.

CLOTHOLD. Well, my lord, if doing what's right is now your watchword, then you won't be offended if I do the same. You would wage war against your father, but I cannot counsel you or come to your aid against my king. I am at your mercy; kill me.

SIGISMUND. Swine! Traitor! Ingrate!

(*Aside.*) But heavens! I should exercise more restraint, for I still don't know if I'm awake.

(*To* CLOTHOLD.) Clothold, I envy and appreciate your valor. Go serve the king, and we'll see each other on the battlefield. (*To his* SOLDIERS.) You there, sound the call to arms.

CLOTHOLD. (*Rising.*) You have my eternal gratitude. (*Exit.*)

SIGISMUND. Off we go, fortune, to restore my reign. Don't wake me if I'm sleeping, and don't put me to sleep if it's real. Yet, whether it's reality or a dream, doing what's right is what matters. If it's reality, then for the sake of reality;

if it's a dream, then for the purpose of winning friends for when we awaken. *(Exit all amid the call to arms.)*

SCENE 2 (VV. 2428–2655). KING'S PALACE.

Enter VASILY *and* AISTULF.

VASILY. Who, Aistulf, is wise enough to curb the fury of a runaway horse? Who can detain the current of an imperious river in its downhill rush to the sea? Who is courageous enough to stay a boulder that has broken free of the mountaintop? Well, that's all easy in comparison to halting a willful and reckless mob. The proof is in the clashing cries of Poland's rival parties, which fill the mountains with thunderous echoes of "Long live Aistulf!" or "Long live Sigismund!" *(The voices indicated are heard offstage.)* The coronation site, fallen prey to wayward aspirations and hidden loyalties, has become a gloomy theater where importunate fortune stages her tragedies.

AISTULF. We must stay the celebration, my lord, and postpone the acclaim and flattering delights your favored hand promised me; for if Poland, which I hope to rule, today refuses obedience to me, it is to make me earn it first. Give me a horse and watch as I turn my arrogant thunder into a bolt of lightning. *(Exit.)*

VASILY. The inevitable has little remedy, and the foreseeable carries considerable risk; if it's meant to be, there's no defense against it, for trying to avoid it only precipitates its arrival. What harsh logic! What extreme circumstances! What tremendous horror! He who thinks he's running from danger ends up running into it. My attempts to forestall fate have ruined me. I, and I alone, have destroyed my fatherland.

Enter STELLA.

STELLA. If you do not act quickly, Your Majesty, to put a stop to the chaos that has broken out and, spreading from one side to the next, polarizes streets and squares, you will soon find your kingdom swimming in waves of scarlet, drenched in the crimson of its own blood. Sorrow is already widespread as misfortune and tragedy take hold. Such is the ruin of your empire, such the might of harsh and bloody strife that it amazes the eyes and shocks the ears.

The sun reels in confusion and the wind stifles its breezes; every rock is a tombstone and every flower marks a grave; every building is a mausoleum and every soldier a living skeleton.

Enter CLOTHOLD.

CLOTHOLD. Thank God I've made it here alive!

VASILY. Clothold! What can you tell us of Sigismund?

CLOTHOLD. A monstrous mob, impulsive and blind, broke into the tower and liberated the prince from its depths. Finding his power seconded a second time, he became courageous, proclaiming fiercely that he would prove the heavens right.

VASILY. Give me a horse, and I, ever courageous, shall defeat my ungrateful son face to face. In the defense of my crown, may steel triumph where learning has failed. *(Exit.)*

STELLA. And I, flanking the sun *(Gesturing toward* VASILY *as he exits.)*, shall act as Bellona. I hope to write my name next to yours, for I shall fly on loyal wings in competition with Pallas. *(Exit amid the call to arms.)*

Enter ROSSAURA, *who detains* CLOTHOLD.

ROSSAURA. I realize we're in the midst of war, but even if your heart is bursting with valor in its desire to aid the king, hear me out. You know that I arrived in Poland poor, humble, and unfortunate and that, aided by your stature, I found refuge in your devotion. You ordered me—oh, heavens!—to live in disguise in the palace and to attempt, concealing my jealousy, to keep away from Aistulf. But he saw me in the end, and he has so little respect for my honor that he speaks to Stella in front of me every night in the garden. I've stolen the key, with which you can enter the garden and put an end to my troubles. Willful, bold, and adamant, you can affirm my honor there since you're already resolved to avenge me with his death.

CLOTHOLD. It's true that from the moment I met you, Rossaura, I was moved by your sobs to do for you whatever my life allowed. The first thing I did was to get you to change that outfit you were wearing so that, if Aistulf saw you, he'd see you in your own clothes and not take for indecency the mad temerity that besmirches honor. I've since been trying to determine how to recover your lost honor even if it meant—so much does your honor preoccupy me!—killing Aistulf. What futile madness! Although, given that he's not my king, I'm neither frightened nor awed by him. I was planning to kill him when Sigismund tried to kill me, and just then he showed up and, overlooking all danger to himself, demonstrated a degree of altruism in my defense that went past courage to temerity. So tell me, how am I now to kill the person who saved my life when my soul is full of gratitude? And thus, with appreciation on one side and affection on the other, having given you life and received it from him, I don't know which party to attend to or to help; for to you I'm bound on account of giving, and to him I'm bound on account of receiving. And thus, in the matter at hand, there's no way to satisfy my heart because my active and passive tempers are at odds.

ROSSAURA. I needn't remind you that, in men of exception, receiving is as base an act as giving is noble. Accepting this principle, you have no reason to be grateful to him given that, if he gave you life and you gave it to me, it's obvious that he forced your noble nature to commit a base act while I facilitated its generosity. Therefore you should consider yourself offended by him and indebted to me, for you have given to me what you received from him. And thus you should attend to my honor, which is at great risk, for it gives me precedence in the conflict between giving and receiving.

CLOTHOLD. Although nobility lives in those who give, gratitude for noble actions corresponds to those who receive. And as I have not held back in giving, my honorable name has become identified with generosity. Let me now become known as grateful, for I can do so while still being charitable, for giving and receiving are equally honorable.

ROSSAURA. You gave me life and, in doing so, said yourself that a life lived in dishonor is no life. Therefore I haven't actually received anything from you, for in reality your hand has dispensed death, not life. And if you must be charitable before grateful—as you just said—I expect you to give me my life, which you haven't done yet; and, since giving is more dignified, be charitable first, and later there will be time to be grateful.

CLOTHOLD. I'm convinced by your reasoning and shall indeed be charitable first. I shall, Rossaura, give you my inheritance, with which you may retire to a convent. This is a good solution to our problem since, in fleeing from a crime, you will take refuge in a sanctuary. For when a divided kingdom is burdened with misfortunes, I don't wish to multiply them, for I was born noble. With this remedy I can be loyal to my country, charitable to you, and grateful to Aistulf. It behooves you to accept this remedy, which we'll keep between the two of us, for I wouldn't do anything more even if—by God!—I were your father.

ROSSAURA. If you were my father, I would accept this insult; but since you're not, I refuse.

CLOTHOLD. Then what do you plan to do?

ROSSAURA. Kill the duke.

CLOTHOLD. Can a lady who never knew her father have such valor?

ROSSAURA. Yes.

CLOTHOLD. What drives you?

ROSSAURA. My reputation.

CLOTHOLD. Beware that Aistulf is about to become . . .

ROSSAURA. My honor trumps all else.

CLOTHOLD. . . . your king and husband to Stella.

ROSSAURA. By God, it shall not happen!

CLOTHOLD. This is madness.

ROSSAURA. I know.

CLOTHOLD. You must overcome it.

ROSSAURA. I cannot.

CLOTHOLD. You'll lose . . .

ROSSAURA. I know.

CLOTHOLD. . . . your life and your honor.

ROSSAURA. I know.

CLOTHOLD. Then what's your goal?

ROSSAURA. My death.

CLOTHOLD. That's sacrilege.

ROSSAURA. It's honorable.

CLOTHOLD. It's absurd.

ROSSAURA. It's valiant.

CLOTHOLD. It's reckless.

ROSSAURA. It's the product of rage and ire.

CLOTHOLD. So there's no compromising with your blind frenzy?

ROSSAURA. No.

CLOTHOLD. Who will help you?

ROSSAURA. I'll help myself.

CLOTHOLD. There's no other solution?

ROSSAURA. There's no other solution.

CLOTHOLD. Think about it; there must be another way.

ROSSAURA. Only another form of self-destruction. *(Exit.)*

CLOTHOLD. Well, if you're bent on destroying yourself, wait for me, my daughter, and we'll go down together. *(Exit.)*

SCENE 3 (VV. 2656–3319). A WILDERNESS AREA,
SOMEWHERE BETWEEN THE PALACE AND THE TOWER.

Amid the call to arms, SOLDIERS, BUGLE, *and* SIGISMUND *march out, the latter dressed in animal skins.*

SIGISMUND. If Rome at her most triumphant could see me today, how thrilled she would be at the rare opportunity of having her mighty armies led by a beast whose headstrong vigor strikes at the firmament itself! But let's come back to earth, my spirit. We mustn't exalt this tenuous acclaim if I'll be disappointed upon waking at having achieved so much only to lose it; for the lesser the acclaim, the less it will be missed if it's lost.

A bugle sounds offstage.

BUGLE. We are approached by a swift horse—forgive me, but its description requires considerable detail—upon which a careful map is drawn in which the body is formed of earth, the soul is made up of fire trapped in the chest, the frothy mouth partakes of the sea, and air is exhaled in its hot breath; the motley figure inspires chaos, for its body, soul, frothy mouth, and breath form a monster of earth, fire, sea, and wind. Upon its coarse coat of dapple gray sits a remarkable woman who, in seeking your presence, digs in the spurs and bids it fly rather than gallop.

SIGISMUND. Her aura is blinding.

BUGLE. By God, it's Rossaura! *(Exit.)*

SIGISMUND. Heaven has restored her to my presence.

Enter ROSSAURA *with a splendid cloak, a sword, and a dagger.*

ROSSAURA. Kind Sigismund, shining sun of Poland, whose heroic majesty is emerging into the day of its deeds from the night of its nothingness; may your ascent in the world be like that of the greatest of heavenly bodies, which, in the arms of dawn, recovers its shining throne among flowers and roses and, stepping out newly crowned, spreads light and casts rays over oceans and mountains, bathing high peaks and adorning frothy waves. Grant refuge to this unlucky woman who today throws herself at your feet, who, being both unfortunate and a woman, has two reasons to expect charity from a man who prides himself on his courage—either of which is enough, either of which is more than enough. Three times now you have beheld me, three times without knowing who I am, for on each occasion you've seen me in different attire and surroundings. The first time was in your cruel prison, where you took me for a man and your life made my misfortunes seem flattering. The second time—when you saw your majestic splendor reduced to a dream, a ghost, a shadow—you beheld me as a woman. The third time is today, where, like a monstrous hybrid, I mix the fine clothes of a woman with the weapons of a man. And so that pity may move you to act on my behalf, listen to the tragic events of my life. I was born at court in Muscovy to a noble mother who, to judge from her misfortunes, must have been quite beautiful. She caught the eye of a treacherous scoundrel, whom I don't name because I don't know him, although my own valor tells me something of his; and, as the product of his inclinations, I regret now not being born pagan so that I could madly convince myself that he was one of those gods who—transformed into a shower of gold, a swan, or a bull—are lamented by <u>Danae</u>, <u>Leda</u>, and <u>Europa</u>. Although I thought these two-timing tales would simply embellish my speech, I realize now that they sum up perfectly what I wish to tell you: that my mother, swept away in the game of love, was more beautiful than any other woman and as unlucky as all of them. She was so completely duped by that foolish old ruse of a secret wedding vow that she relives it even today; and her betrayer was so like <u>Aeneas</u> fleeing from responsibility that he even left her a sword. Its blade will remain covered for now, but I shall unsheathe it before my story is over. From this poorly tied knot that neither binds nor imprisons, from this secret wedding vow or wicked lie—for it's all the same—I was born, so similar to my mother that I could have passed for her double, if not in loveliness then in luck and circumstances. And thus I needn't say that her stormy fortune ran me through many shipwrecks of my own. The most I can tell you is the name of the lord who robs my honor and sacks my reputation: Aistulf. Oh, miserable me! At the mere mention of his name my heart fills with anger and bile, chafing at any allusion to the enemy. Aistulf was the ungrateful lord who, forgetting our shared pleasure—for when love is extinguished, all memories are forgotten—came to Poland, lured by his ambition, to marry Stella, his north star and my setting sun. Who would have guessed that, having been brought together through stellar design, we would now be separated by Stella's design? The humiliating offense left me sad, demented, and dead, yet still myself; that is to say, I felt the confusion of hell and the chaos of <u>Babylonia</u>

in my soul. And refusing to talk about it, because some sufferings and anguish are much better left to feelings than to words, I spoke my sufferings in silence until one day, when I was alone with my mother Viola—oh, heavens!—she broke them free of their prison, and they all poured out together, tripping over one another in their haste. I didn't try to keep them in, for when a person confesses his faults to someone he knows has similar faults, he feels free and uninhibited in doing so, for there are times when a bad example does some good. In any case, my mother listened devotedly to my laments and tried to console me with her own. How easily a guilty judge forgives! And learning a lesson from her own experience—whereby, having entrusted the remedy of her dishonor to idle liberty and lenient time, she now had no way to remedy my own misfortunes—she considered it best that I go after the duke and obligate him, with overpowering arguments, to pay the debt of my honor; and to make it easier, fortune had her dress me in the clothes of a man. She took down an old sword—this one you see me wearing. Now's the time to unsheathe it as I promised, for my mother, trusting in its unique appearance, said to me: "Make your way to Poland, Rossaura, and do your best to have the nobles there see you wearing this sword, for in one of them your fortunes may find a merciful welcome and your anguish, consolation." Thus I arrived in Poland. I'll quickly summarize what needn't be repeated in detail because it's already known: that a bucking beast led me to your cave, where you were astonished to see me; that Clothold took pity on me, asked the king for my life, and the king granted his request; that Clothold, informed of my identity, persuaded me to wear my normal clothes and enter the service of Stella, where I ingeniously thwarted Aistulf's courtship and marriage to her; that there, in the palace, you were again baffled at the sight of me, this time dressed as a woman, my past and present appearances confused in your mind; and finally, that Clothold, convinced of the importance that Aistulf marry the lovely Stella and rule jointly with her, advised me to forget my dishonor and end my crusade. But now, O valiant Sigismund, that your turn at revenge has arrived, for heaven has allowed you to break free of that crude prison cell where sorrow made your soul savage and suffering made it unyielding; now that you are taking up arms against your fatherland and against your father, I am here to offer my help, combining the rich garments of <u>Diana</u> and the arms of <u>Pallas</u>—cloth here and steel there—for I am at home in both. Let's move quickly then, brave chief! For we both have an interest in preventing or annulling this arranged marriage: I, to stop the man who promised to marry me from marrying another; you, to preempt the threat to our victory that the strength and power of their two states, once united, would represent. As a woman, I come to move you to the cause of my honor; as a man, I come to encourage you to recover your crown. As a woman, I come to beg your sympathy by throwing myself at your feet; as a man, I come to serve you by aiding your soldiers. As a woman, I come to request your support in my dishonor and anguish; as a man, I come to support you with my sword and my character. And finally, consider that if you try to seduce me today as a woman, as a man I will slay you in legitimate defense of my honor; for in restoring my good name I must act as a lovesick woman to plead for help and as a man to win respect.

SIGISMUND. *(Aside.)* Heavens, if I'm really dreaming, then stay my memory, for it's impossible for a dream to have so many twists and turns! God help me! Who could manage to escape them all or avoid thinking about any of them? Who ever heard of such baffling torments? If that grandeur in which I awoke was a dream, how is it that this woman can now describe it to me in such vivid detail? So it had to be real, not a dream. But if it was real, it's no less confusing, for why does my experience call it a dream? Are pleasures so akin to dreams that the real ones are taken for lies and the fake ones for authentic? Is there so little difference between the true and the false that it's debatable whether what is seen and enjoyed is real or made up? Is the copy so close to the original that it can pass inspection undetected? If so, and all grandeur and power, all majesty and splendor will eventually fade into shadow, then we must take advantage of this moment while we can, for it affords us enjoyment to be found only in dreams. Rossaura is in my power; my soul longs for her loveliness. Let's enjoy, then, the occasion and permit love to violate the ideals of valor and trust with which she kneels before me. This is a dream, and, that being the case, let's dream of joys now, for they're sure to become sorrows later. *(Pause.)* But my own argument can be used against me. If it's a dream, a show, who would risk losing divine glory for the sake of human vainglory? What past good is not a dream? Who has never thought, when he looks back on his heroic achievements, "It must have all been a dream"? If this is my lesson, if I know that delight is a lovely flame and will be reduced to ashes by the first breeze that blows, then we must focus on the eternal, where fame is everlasting, joy never sleeps, and grandeur never rests. Rossaura is without honor, and a prince's responsibility is to dispense honor rather than to rob it. By God, I shall restore her honor before my own crown! But first, we must turn our back on this temptation. *(He struggles to divert his gaze from* ROSSAURA.*)*

(To a SOLDIER.*)* Sound the call to arms, for today I must do battle before the dark shadows bury the sun's golden rays in waves of greenish black!

ROSSAURA. My lord, are you going to leave just like that? My worries and anguish don't merit a single word from you in reply? How can you not even look at me or listen to me? You won't even show me your face?

SIGISMUND. *(Without looking at her.)* Rossaura, honor demands that I be cruel to you now in order to be merciful later. My voice is silent so my honor may respond; I don't speak to you because I want my actions to speak for me; I don't look at you because it's essential, when your cruel suffering makes you so vulnerable, that he who is to look after your honor not look upon your beauty.

Exit SIGISMUND *and* SOLDIERS.

ROSSAURA. What enigmatic talk is this, heavens? After so much sorrow, must I still put up with ambivalent responses?

Enter BUGLE.

BUGLE. My lady, do you have a moment?

ROSSAURA. Oh, Bugle! Where have you been?

BUGLE. Locked away in a tower wondering what the cards had in store for me and when I might be put to death, for they could have knocked me off at any moment.

ROSSAURA. Why?

BUGLE. Because I know the secret of your identity. You see . . .

Offstage, the drums of war are heard.

BUGLE. . . . Clothold . . . but what's all that racket?

ROSSAURA. What could it be?

BUGLE. An armed squadron is spilling out of the besieged palace in hopes of resisting and defeating the regiment commanded by the fierce Sigismund.

ROSSAURA. Well, how can I stand here like a coward when such cruelty is unleashed without order or rules? I must fight by his side and astound the world. *(Exit.)*

SOLDIERS. *(Offstage, one group.)* Long live our invincible king! *(Offstage, another group.)* Long live our freedom!

BUGLE. I say long live freedom *and* the king. Let them live with my blessing, for I have no problem with either as long as they look out for me. And now, amid such confusion, I must withdraw and be as pitiless as Nero as he watched Rome burn. Although I'd like to take pity on something, so it might as well be on me; if I hide, I can watch the whole spectacle from here among the crags. It's a safe place where death won't find me, so to hell with death! *(He makes an obscene gesture, directed at death, and hides.)*

The sound of clashing arms becomes stronger. Enter VASILY, CLOTHOLD, *and* AISTULF, *in retreat.*

VASILY. Has there ever been an unluckier king? Has there ever been a more persecuted father?

CLOTHOLD. Your army, now defeated, retreats in disorder.

AISTULF. The traitors have won.

VASILY. In battles such as this, the winners always consider themselves loyal and treat the losers as traitors. We must flee, Clothold, from the cruel and inhuman severity of a tyrannical son.

A shot is heard offstage, and BUGLE *falls down, wounded, from his hiding place.*

BUGLE. Heaven help me!

AISTULF. Who is this unlucky soldier who has fallen at our feet, drenched in blood?

BUGLE. Just an unfortunate man who, in trying to run from death, ran right into her, for there's no hiding place she can't find. Which goes to show that he who most tries to flee from her reach is the one who will first fall within her reach. So return, return to the bloody fighting immediately, for you're safer amid arms and open fire than on the most shielded mountaintop, and there's no road that will protect you against the power of destiny and the inclemency of fate. And thus, although you hope to free yourselves from death by fleeing, consider that, if it's God's will that you die, then you shall die. *(He dies.)*

VASILY. "Consider that, if it's God's will that you die, then you shall die." How easily—oh, heavens!—we are brought from error and ignorance to greater understanding by this corpse that speaks through the mouth of an open wound, its hemorrhage a bloody tongue that teaches us that all attempts to cheat fate are in vain; for I, in attempting to save my fatherland from sedition and death, have in the end turned it over to the very people from whom I was attempting to save it!

CLOTHOLD. Although fate, my lord, sees all and is capable of finding its prey in even the darkest crags, it isn't of Christian temperament to conclude that there's no way around its wrath. There is, and a prudent man can triumph over fate; and now, if you wish to avoid further suffering and tragedy, you should find a place where you can protect yourself.

AISTULF. Clothold, my lord, speaks with the wisdom of old age and I with the courage of youth. Over there in the thicket stands a horse, swift miscarriage of the wind; use it to flee, and I shall guard your back.

VASILY. If it's God's will that I die or if death already awaits me here, today I shall seek her out and confront her face to face.

The call to arms is sounded, and SIGISMUND *enters accompanied by his* SOLDIERS.

SOLDIER 1. Among the crags and thickets of the mountain hides the king.

SIGISMUND. Seek him out! I want every tree and shrub of these jagged peaks scrutinized, trunk by trunk and branch by branch!

CLOTHOLD. *(To* VASILY.*)* Flee, my lord!

VASILY. To what end?

AISTULF. What are you going to do?

VASILY. Step aside, Aistulf!

CLOTHOLD. What are you going to do?

VASILY. The only thing I haven't yet tried, Clothold. *(To* SIGISMUND.*)* If I'm the one you're looking for, you have me at your mercy, my prince. *(He kneels before* SIGISMUND *and remains on his knees throughout the prince's reply.)* Use the snow of my hair as a white rug beneath your feet; trample my neck and tread upon my crown; humiliate me and drag my good name through the mud; take your vengeance on my honor and treat me as your captive. After so many warnings, fate shall honor its promise and heaven shall keep its word.

SIGISMUND. Illustrious Court of Poland, witness to so many amazing events, listen carefully, for your prince wishes to address you. What is determined by heaven from the blue slate inscribed by the finger of God—and encoded and printed on those immense blue spheres adorned with gold stars—never deceives or lies; the lies and deceptions come from the one who, wishing to use the information to his own ends, undertakes to decipher it. My father, who is present among us, in order to avoid the wrath of my character, turned me into a brute, a human beast; thus, whereas my graceful nobility, genteel lineage, and fine character should have made me congenial and humble, my living conditions and upbringing were sufficient to cultivate a ferocious disposition. What a way to cheat fate! If anyone were told, "One day you will be killed by an inhuman beast," would it be a good solution to wake one up while it was sleeping? If they said, "That sword you're wearing will one day be the death of you," to then take it out and point it at your chest would prove a futile remedy. If they said, "Your grave will lie beneath vast expanses of water and bear tombstones of silvery waves," you would be foolish to set sail when the imperious sea was whipping up rough, jagged mountains of snow and glass. My father has ended up just like the one who, threatened by a beast, woke it up; like the one who, fearful of the sword, unsheathed it; and like the one who stirred up the waves of a tempest. And even if—and listen well—my wrath were a dormant beast, my fury a dull sword, and my severity a gentle tropical breeze, fortune is not to be overcome through injustice and vengeance but rather is provoked even further by such measures. Whoever wishes to overcome his fortune must do so through prudence and temperance. Foreseeing a danger doesn't mean you can protect yourself or guard against it before it occurs; yes, you can always take a few humble measures to protect yourself, but not until the moment is upon you, for there's no way of forestalling its arrival. Of this there's no better proof than the strange spectacle we've witnessed today: this bizarre, amazing event, this horrific aberration. Just look and you'll see—despite all efforts to the contrary—a father vanquished, a monarch crushed before my feet. This was the work of heaven, and no matter how he tried to prevent it, he was unable. But I—inferior to him in years, valor, and learning—shall succeed where he failed. Rise, my lord, and give me your hand; now that heaven has revealed the error in your attempts to overcome it, my neck humbly awaits your vengeance. I am at your mercy.

VASILY. My son, such noble action rekindles your presence in my heart. You are prince! The laurel and the palm are yours; let your deeds be your crown.

ALL. *(In unison.)* Long live Sigismund! Long live Sigismund!

Enter ROSSAURA.

SIGISMUND. *(Observing* ROSSAURA.*)* My valor promises me great victories, and today the greatest of all will be victory over myself. Aistulf, promise your hand to Rossaura immediately, for you know you're a debtor to her honor, and I intend to make you pay.

AISTULF. Although it's true I owe her something, bear in mind that she doesn't know who her father is; and it would be a low and infamous deed for someone like me to marry a woman who . . .

CLOTHOLD. Do not go on; hold your tongue and listen. Rossaura is just as noble as you, Aistulf, and I will argue her case with my sword if I have to. She is my daughter, and that's all you need to know.

AISTULF. What are you saying?

CLOTHOLD. Until I saw her promised in noble marriage and her honor avenged, I didn't want to reveal the secret. It's a very long story, but the point is that she's my daughter.

AISTULF. Well, that being the case, I shall honor my word. *(He takes* ROSSAURA'S *hand.)*

SIGISMUND. And now, so that Stella won't feel left out given that she's lost a prince of such valor and reputation, by my own hand I shall wed her to a man who is, in merits and good fortune, if not greater than Aistulf, at least his equal. Give me your hand, my lady. *(He takes* STELLA'S *hand.)*

STELLA. I'm honored to be worthy of such joy.

SIGISMUND. To Clothold, who was unswerving in his loyalty to my father, I offer my warm embrace together with any favors he might ask of me.

SOLDIER 1. If that's how you reward someone who never came to your aid, what do I get for inciting the uprising against the king and for freeing you from the tower in which you were imprisoned?

SIGISMUND. The tower. And so that you'll spend the rest of your life there, you'll be under constant watch of the guards, for traitors serve no purpose once their treason has been exposed.

VASILY. Your ingenuity amazes us all.

AISTULF. What a change of character!

ROSSAURA. What discretion, what prudence!

SIGISMUND. What's so amazing, what's so shocking, given that my teacher was a dream? And I still fear, deep down inside, that one day I shall awaken to find myself locked away in my cramped prison. And if that doesn't happen, it's enough to dream it's so, for that's how I came to realize that all human joy is, in the end, as ephemeral as a dream. So I'd like to take advantage of this happy moment while I can . . . *(To the audience.)* and ask you to overlook our flaws, for forgiveness should come naturally to noble souls.

Glossary

Note: I believe all these terms will be comprehensible in performance in the contexts in which I have translated them. For directors who disagree, I offer in brackets acceptable substitutions for the most obscure entries.

Aeneas. Trojan hero of Virgil's epic poem, the *Aeneid;* son of Anchises and Aphrodite. He escaped the sack of Troy and wandered for seven years before settling in Italy. Book 4 of the *Aeneid* recounts how he stops in Carthage (near present-day Tunis), where the queen, Dido, falls in love with him; but he is convinced by the gods to abandon her in order to pursue his destiny as the founder of Rome. He leaves behind a sword, and the queen, overwhelmed by grief, stabs herself with it and hurls herself onto a funeral pyre.

Atlas. In Greek mythology, a Titan condemned by Zeus to support the heavens on his shoulders. Calderón often refers to him as a metaphor for those who support the elderly. [Atlas-like ⟶ supportive]

Aurora. Roman personification of the dawn who came to be identified with the Greek goddess Eos. Aurora is seen as a lovely woman who flies across the sky announcing the arrival of the sun. According to one myth, her tears cause the dew as she flies across the sky weeping for a slain son. [Dawn]

Babylonia. Ancient empire of Mesopotamia in the Euphrates River valley with its capital at Babylon. It flourished under Hammurabi and Nebuchadnezzar II but declined after 562 B.C. and fell to the Persians in 539. In Calderón, it was a symbol of chaos because of its associations with the Tower of Babel.

Bellona. Roman goddess of war, popular among Roman soldiers. Her attribute is the sword, and she is depicted wearing a helmet and armed with a spear and a torch. She accompanied Mars in battle and was variously understood as his wife, sister, or daughter; but Calderón identifies her with the sun, meant to represent the king. ["act as Bellona" ⟶ "fight with ferocity"]

Danae. In Greek mythology, the daughter of Acrisius. An oracle warned her father that Danae's son would someday kill him, so Acrisius shut Danae in a bronze room, away from male company. However, Zeus conceived a passion for her and came to her through the roof in the form of a shower of gold that poured down into her lap; as a result she had a son, Perseus, who eventually fulfilled the prophecy by killing Acrisius. ["Danae, Leda, Europa" ⟶ "those who fell for such ruses"]

Diana. In Roman mythology, the virgin goddess of hunting and childbirth, traditionally associated with the moon and identified with the Greek Artemis. Calderón seems to want to contrast her to the warlike Pallas, perhaps because of the nurturing qualities associated with midwives, but her virginity and her role as huntress blur the opposition. In the Zaragoza branch of the play's textual transmission, "Venus" appears in place of "Diana" at this point in the manuscript. [Venus]

Dropsy. Medical condition, known in modern times as edema, characterized by abnormal accumulation of fluid in the body tissues or body cavities, causing swelling or distention of the affected parts. In the Renaissance it was thought to be caused by excess drinking, so further intake of liquids was considered life threatening. ["suffer from the dropsy" ⟶ "be insatiable"]

Euclid. Greek mathematician of the third century B.C. who applied the deductive principles of logic to geometry, thereby deriving statements from clearly defined axioms. Calderón's reference to him is an example of *antonomasia*, that is, the use of a well-known proper name to represent an entire group (in this case, mathematicians). [mathematician]

Europa. In Greek mythology, a Phoenician princess who inflamed the desire of Zeus. He appeared to her in the form of a beautiful white bull and encountered her at the seashore. By appearing to be tame, he coaxed her to climb onto his back and then swam off with her across the sea to Crete. The so-called "rape of Europa" is a favorite motif of Renaissance poetry and iconography. [For substitutions, see **Danae.**]

Flora. Roman goddess of the blossoming flowers of spring. [Springtime]

Halberd. Weapon of the fifteenth and sixteenth centuries that came to replace the lance in combat, having an axlike blade and a steel spike mounted on the end of a long shaft. Halberds are still brandished today by the Swiss Guard at the Vatican. [halberd-brandishing ⟶ well-armed]

Henbane. Poisonous Eurasian plant (*Hyoscyamus niger*) having an unpleasant odor, sticky leaves, and funnel-shaped greenish-yellow flowers. Its effects are similar to those of belladonna, which causes deep sleep, delirium, euphoria, and hallucinations. When combined with opium as in the cocktail Sigismund is made to drink, the effect is heightened, bordering on hysteria or schizophrenia. [belladonna]

Hippogriff. Fabulous beast popularized in Ariosto's *Orlando furioso* (1532). The hippogriff has the body and hindquarters of a horse and the wings, claws, and head of a griffin (itself a mythological monster with the head, wings, and talons of an eagle and the body of a lion). As the first word in the Spanish version of the play, the hippogriff alludes to the swiftness of the horse that has just thrown Rossaura; more important, it is a central metaphor that represents the half-man, half-beast nature of Sigismund and foreshadows the chaos and confusion into which the country is about to plunge. See Introduction, pp. 36–37, for a discussion. [chimera]

Icarus. In Greek mythology, the son of Daedalus who, in escaping from Crete on artificial wings his father made for him, flew so close to the sun that the wax with which his wings were fastened melted; he fell to his death in the Aegean Sea. Bugle refers to him in allusion to the servant thrown off the balcony by Sigismund. [little Icarus ⟶ the servant]

Leda. In Greek mythology, queen of Sparta who, seduced by Zeus in the form of a swan, laid an egg from which hatched the twins Castor and Pollux. [For substitutions, see **Danae.**]

Lysippus. Greek sculptor, head of the school of Argos and Sicyon in the time of Alexander the Great (fourth century B.C.). His works are said to have numbered 1,500, some of them colossal, but nothing of his own hand is known to have survived. Calderón may have been familiar with him through Alexander's famous edict that no one carve him in stone but Lysippus. [Michelangelo]

Nero. Emperor of Rome (54–68), whose cruelty and recklessness provoked widespread revolts and ultimately led to his suicide. He was widely synonymous with tyranny in the Renaissance, and Bugle's allusion springs from a long tradition that blamed him (probably unjustly) for intentionally starting the disastrous fire of A.D. 64 and then calmly playing music as the city burned. Cf. Shakespeare: "Plantagenet, I will—and like thee, Nero, / Play on the lute, beholding the towns burn" (*1 Henry VI* 1.6.73–74).

New Calendar. The Gregorian Calendar, which, by mandate of Pope Gregory XIII, replaced the Julian Calendar throughout Catholic Europe in 1582. (Its implementation was resisted in Protestant Europe until the eighteenth century and in Eastern Orthodox countries until the twentieth century.) When the reform was implemented, ten days were taken out of October so that the fourteenth followed the fourth. The change caused great confusion, of which people apparently took advantage in order to cut out fasting days from religious celebrations. In the passage in question, Bugle is in the opposite situation because he fasts and never feasts.

Pallas. Title of the goddess Athena (Pallas Athena), who, according to some accounts, was the daughter of the Titan Pallas. In Greek mythology, Pallas Athena was a virgin goddess of wisdom, war, the arts, industry, justice, and skill; but Calderón alludes to her primarily in reference to her role in war. [Athena]

Phaëthon. In Greek mythology, the son of the sun god Helios. He induced his father to allow him to drive the chariot of the sun across the heavens for one day. The horses, feeling their reins held by a weaker hand, ran wildly off their course and came close to the earth, threatening to burn it. Zeus noticed the danger and destroyed Phaëthon with a thunderbolt. In Calderón (who wrote a play based on this myth), he is a symbol of rash arrogance. [ill-fated leader]

Seneca, Lucius Annaeus. C. 4 B.C. to A.D. 65. Known as "the Younger." Roman Stoic philosopher, writer, and tutor of Nero. His works include treatises on rhetoric and governance and numerous plays that influenced Renaissance drama. Born in what is now Spain (the Roman province Hispania), he was a favorite of classical Spanish authors including Calderón.

Shawm. Medieval wind instrument, forerunner of the modern oboe. [oboe]

Syncopate. In grammar, to shorten a word by omitting a sound, letter, or syllable from the middle. Thus, to "syncopate the light of day" would mean to obliterate the sun. [truncate]

Thales. Greek thinker (c. 624–546 B.C.), a founder of geometry and abstract astronomy, and traditionally considered the first Western philosopher. He maintained that matter is composed of water and, most important in the context of *Life's a Dream,* accurately predicted a solar eclipse in 585 B.C. Calderón's reference to him is another instance of antonomasia (see entry for **Euclid**), in this case meaning astrologer. [astrologer]

Timanthes. A celebrated Greek painter who flourished in Sicyon around 400 B.C. and whose masterpiece was a famous picture of the sacrifice of Iphigenia. He seems to have represented classical painting par excellence for Calderón. [Leonardo]